Psalms for Praise and Worship

A Complete Liturgical Psalter
(Psalms 1-150)

PSALMS
FOR PRAISE AND
WORSHIP

A Complete
Liturgical Psalter

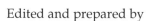

Edited and prepared by

John C. Holbert; S T Kimbrough, Jr.; Carlton R. Young

with Foreword by Walter Brueggemann

Abingdon Press

PSALMS FOR PRAISE AND WORSHIP

Copyright © 1992 by Abingdon Press

First Printing

All Rights Reserved.

ISBN 0-687-09326-0

This book is printed on recycled, acid-free paper.

MANUFACTURED IN THE UNITED STATES OF AMERICA

For Harrell Beck (1922–1987),
Teacher, friend, and lover of the psalms

Foreword

There is currently a great deal of ferment in psalm studies. On the more academic side, attention is being paid to the use and context of the psalms, and to their canonical intentionality. The greater interest, however, concerns the pastoral-liturgical potential of the psalms. On the one hand, that potential has been conceptually available since the magisterial work of Sigmund Mowinckel showed how a "cultic" interpretation of the psalms is possible and productive. On the other hand, however, I suggest that it is our social context and our cultural crisis that evoke attentiveness to pastoral potential issues in the Book of Psalms.

In his rich and daring work on the horrors and inhumanities of the modern world, Robert Jay Lifton has often used the phrase "symbol gap" to characterize the slippage between experienced horror, and the symbols and images adequate to express, process, and appropriate that experience. In an increasingly flat, one-dimensional, media-driven society, "experiences" are not adequately processed, and we miss them in their threat and in their wonder. A very large program of current study concerning human beings as "symbol makers" and "symbol users" has made it clear that in a reductionist, technological society, attentiveness to adequate, reliable symbolization is a *sine qua non* for our future. Indeed, Paul Ricoeur has shown that the use of "limit expression" is decisive if "limit experiences" are to be fully and honestly experienced—that is, without denial and cover-up.

We know, moreover, that such practice of symbolization, upon which our humanness depends, is not an individualized, rational activity, but belongs inescapably to the speaking, listening, and inter-action of concrete communities of interpretation. Or, said in more conventional religious language, human life depends upon communities of worship to provide and enact symbolization. In the Jewish and Christian traditions, it is the psalms that provide the materials, the "script," for such symbolization. This current practical ferment concerns the utilization of the psalms, which contain the most elemental, candid, and daring symbols that we possess to match, shape, and evoke our experiences of depth, from which we live. The "limit expressions" of hymn and complaint in the Book of Psalms permit us to experience the wonder and misery of our time in God's world.

These large interpretive themes, reflected in the work of Lifton, Ricoeur, and many others, converge in a practical, usable way in this book. The three authors, Holbert, Kimbrough, and Young, represent and embody amazing skills, competencies, and sensitivities that include a capacity for scripture study, awareness of the history of psalm usage, skill in music, and long experience in the theory and practice of worship. The outcome of this work is to offer wondrously usable materials for the actual practice of the congregation. The users themselves need not be attentive to, or aware of, all the large hermeneutical issues I have identified. Such users will, nonetheless, be engaged in the rich experience of resymbolization, a major act of resistance and defiance against dehumanization. It is a cliché, of course, to say that liturgy is "the work of the people." Cliché notwithstanding, here is a book that offers tools for "the work," which is to enact our God-given humanness in the presence of God and neighbor. Quite concretely, pastors and congregations using these materials will not be spectators but participants in the voicing of praise and complaint, in order to enact the whole of human life in the presence of God's holiness. The work so well suggested in these psalm settings invites a powerful convergence of the duty of God-ward speech and the delight of a day in God's court . . . far better than a thousand anywhere else (Ps. 84:10)!

Walter Brueggemann
Columbia Theological Seminary
July 9, 1992

Contents

Introduction

The psalms are the hymn book of the temple, synagogue, and church. Within them one finds mention of choirs (Ps. 87), instruments (Ps. 150), and melodies (Ps. 69). They were unquestionably intended for singing and some Jewish and Christian traditions have continued the earliest forms of psalm singing. At the beginning of the twentieth century, however, the singing of the psalms had greatly diminished in the western church, and the average churchgoer was more familiar with the psalms as prose than as sung poetry. Yet, when they are only read publicly, something vital is missing. Music! By the middle of this century a revival of interest in psalm singing had begun that has now blossomed into a broad movement with a literature available to most segments of the church. This revival has drawn and built upon diverse musical repertories and given the psalms new life.

Ancient Songs Sung Anew

The contemporary church has heard the psalmist's summons to "sing a new song to the Lord" (Ps. 98:1). It is clear from the renewed interest in the Book of Psalms that they are songs of the heart and, whether read and sung publicly or privately, they express the joys and needs of people everywhere.

The church of the twentieth century is turning once again to these ancient songs of Israel. It rehearses them, sings them anew, and discovers in them the true source of vitality expressed in (1) worship, (2) prayer, (3) theology, and (4) service. (1) The Hebrew poets were energized with *a sense of worship.* Well-known sentences such as, "O come, let us sing unto the Lord," "I will lift up my eyes to the hills," and "The heavens declare the glory of God" reflect their exuberance and awe before God and creation. (2) The psalmists were *bold in prayer* to make themselves fully vulnerable before God and the community of the faithful—to lay themselves bare, to examine themselves, and to pour out their emotions, passions, desires, perceptions, anger, and love to God. (3) The singers of Israel sang with their heads and hearts, with emotion and understanding. They sang with this *theological certainty:* There is a rock of faith which is sure, no matter what the anxiety, despair, or doubt. They understood what St. Paul articulated many years later to the church at Corinth, "I will sing with the spirit, I will sing with the mind also " (I Cor. 14:15). (4) The songs of the psalmists thrust us into *service*. They convey a sense of historical and social responsibility. When we sing them, we come to know our true identity as God's children of justice, that history is not pointless and justice can reign, that there is a faith and a life to share, that God is at the helm of history and we are a part of its process. So sing the psalmists!

It is not surprising that the revival of psalm singing has been accompanied by a flood of new translations. As in every age, changes in language necessitate new translations of scripture. Furthermore, new linguistic, historical, and archaeological discoveries continue to inform the science of biblical translations. Many new translations of the psalms also reflect concerns for contemporary, poetic, and inclusive language, and those which seek to capture their poetic nature remind the worshiping community that the revealed content of the psalter is poetic.

The compelling reason the psalms have received renewed emphasis in contemporary worship is that they have vitality in every age. In singing and praying them we experience bringing the full spectrum of our thought and emotions to God. If we are concerned with our identity and want to know who we *are,* not merely who we can be or should be—if we want to learn to live with the reality that just persons and causes do not always prosper—if we want to be able to bring *all* our emotions and thought, including anger and mistrust, in an honest expression to God—if we desire to know ourselves—if we want to come into direct contact with God through the assent of faith to God's revelation—sing and pray the psalms!

Whether we are young or old, the psalms make us wise for living and give us strength for dying. They speak to us with vitality because they were born among a *servant* people who believed and taught that God was and is at the center of all that is, and who viewed this life as valuable only as lived in proper relationship to creation and the Creator, who gives life, rules nature, judges and redeems humankind.

There are other reasons why these ancient songs are our songs today. (1) The context of their origin is not unlike our own. They were written for a people who were going through cultural deterioration and military demise. Religious syncretism, social and political turmoil surrounded them. Yet they discovered in the midst of human madness that life is worth living. How did they face national disasters, personal problems, suffering and death, joy and sadness, success and failure? They sang! They sang songs which opened new opportunities for communal and self-fulfillment in God's own world. (2) The words of the psalms have become our words. These Hebrew songs have become our songs. They reach out to us and impart strength for the needs of each moment (e.g., Pss. 23, 100, 139, etc.).

Through the singers of Israel, the contemporary church feels the pulse of the life of faith; the vitality of a congregation may be sensed by the way it sings. The stronger the song, the stronger the vital signs of the congregation.

Psalm Singing Traditions

In the synagogue and early church the psalms were often chanted. One of the oldest forms of psalm singing in the western church is *Gregorian Chant*, which derived many of its melodies from the synagogal traditions. It is sometimes called plainchant and was fully developed by the ninth century. In adding musical sounds to the texts, early Christians followed a practice of Jewish worship which made the psalm texts audible to a large group of worshipers, highlighted the meaning of the text, and enhanced the beauty of poetic diction. The purpose was to draw the worshiper closer to the text, its meaning, and to God.

There are eight psalm tones (or melodies) primary to Gregorian Chant, and one is selected for a psalm according to its mood and rhythm. The tones are comprised essentially of two phrases which balance each other. In its purest form Gregorian Chant is a single, unaccompanied melodic line.

With the publication of the French *Bible de Jerusalem*, 1955 *(The Jerusalem Bible)*, Joseph Gelineau, Jr., S. J., drawing upon Gregorian Chant tradition and yet moving beyond it, developed a psalmody now often called *Gelineau Psalms*. It consists of the psalms of this translation designed for singing by fixing the number of stresses in every line of a psalm. The unique contribution of Gelineau is that he created a psalter which approximated the singing of psalms in the Hebrew Bible. He also attempted to group the verses of a psalm according to sense, in place of arbitrary divisions which met certain musical needs but often ignored meaning.

There is also a fully developed tradition of English-language psalm singing associated with the psalter of *The Book of Common*

Prayer known as *Anglican Chant.* The traditional plainsong psalm tones were a primary source for the first singing of this psalter, dating from the middle of the sixteenth century. As Anglican Chant evolved, improvised accompaniments of the psalm tones were created to support the singing. From this practice evolved four-part psalm singing, a choral use of psalm tones not characteristic of Gregorian Chant. By the mid-eighteenth century Anglican Chant was normative wherever the psalms were sung in the Church of England.

In early colonial America metrical psalm singing was much more prevalent than Anglican Chant, and the psalms were usually recited for Morning and Evening Prayer rather than sung. By the mid-nineteenth century, with the revival of sung choral services in many Episcopal churches, there was a parallel revival of singing the psalms to plainsong tones. In this century The Episcopal Church has revived the simple Gregorian melodies of the Daily Office in a responsorial style and has included psalms to be sung at the Eucharist, which has encouraged a revival of psalm singing. The *Lutheran Book of Worship* (1978) also uses the psalter of *The Book of Common Prayer* (1979), printed in a poetic format to be sung to the traditional eight psalm tones but adds two additional tones. The ten psalm tones from the *Lutheran Book of Worship* (1978) are used in this volume (see pages 235-237).

The continental Reformation spawned a plethora of vernacular psalters. Martin Luther and John Calvin stressed psalm singing in their liturgies. The psalters resulting from the Reformation were often *metrical*—that is, the texts were rhymed translations or paraphrases in specific poetical meters. They were joined with newly composed and/or popular tunes. The result was a "hymnic" psalmody. Particularly memorable are "A mighty fortress is our God" (Ps. 46), "Praise, my soul, the King of heaven" (Ps. 103), "The Lord's my shepherd, I'll not want" (Ps. 23), and "O for a heart to praise my God" (Ps. 51).

Metrical psalm singing had a tremendous impact on English language psalmody, and indirectly on hymnody, in terms of texts and tunes and is still popular today, as evidenced by recent hymnals and other publications.

Psalms for Praise and Worship
A Responsorial Psalter

The psalter presented here acknowledges that the psalms are not a series of chapters to be read in isolation. Rather, they create a hymn-book for recitation and singing by the people of God. This version is intended for corporate worship, for congregational reading and singing. The core of the psalm texts used here is the *New Revised Standard Version* of the Bible (1990), which has been prepared by the editors of this volume for public worship with additional translation from Hebrew texts and a concern for the veracity of the English rendering, readability, singability, comprehension, and inclusive language for God and the assembly.

A. Format

The format of the text is *responsorial*, or call and response. There are many speakers in the Book of Psalms—God, the psalmists, the people, evildoers, etc. There are also shifts of persons or speakers within psalms. Sometimes there is even a change in the first, second, or third person of the verb within a psalm. This can make for troublesome and awkward reading, if not carefully formatted. Merely alternating verses in public reading does not in such instances necessarily enhance comprehension of the text nor create sensible choral speech; rather, it often impedes them. Also, at times the many speakers of the psalms heighten the drama within a psalm. Therefore a serious attempt has been made in formatting the text in light and bold face to assist readers in the creation of effective choral speech, which will help a congregation enter the spirit of a psalm and become empowered by its language and message.

Some psalms have their own refrains (see Pss. 8, 42, 43, 46, 67, 136), and these usually function best when read by the congregation. There are psalms in which the cascading impact of the thought(s) expressed is best achieved in corporate reading by alternation of individual lines of verses between leader and congregation or groups of readers.

Parallelism is a characteristic feature of Hebrew poetry that is extremely important to the format of the psalms for public reading. Parallelism identifies two parallel lines of verse, in which the second line has varying functions: It may reflect the idea of the first line but express it differently, stand in direct contrast to the first line, or develop its thought. The role of parallelism has been carefully taken into account for corporate reading.

An attempt has been made to capture the sense of the text, its flow of thought, and to create a format for effective choral speech in the format employed here.

B. The Response

In the synagogue and early church the psalms were often chanted. It was customary in ancient chant for a congregation to sing "Amen" or "Alleluia" at the conclusion of each verse or after the final verse of a psalm. As the liturgy of the church evolved, these congregational responses were extended to developed melodies and became known as *antiphons* (refrains or responses). The texts used for the antiphon were usually psalm quotations, such as "God's steadfast love endures forever," which is the response after each verse of Psalm 136. As the style of psalm singing developed in the church, the antiphons were generally sung only at the beginning and the end of a psalm.

In *Psalms for Praise and Worship* the word *response* is used as a synonym and substitute for *antiphon*. There is, however, historically a difference between the use of antiphons as already described and their use as responses. Antiphons were generally employed at the beginning and the end of the Canticles (biblical songs such as the Song of Mary [Lk. 1:46b-55]), which are not included here. In their usage with psalms antiphons not only preceded and concluded a psalm but were often used as responses at designated places during the repetition of a psalm, or sometimes after each verse. Since this responsorial style is normative for *Psalms for Praise and Worship*, they are designated simply as *responses*.

The responses of this psalter combine many elements of past psalmody. They are sung at the beginning and end of a psalm and also within the repetition of the psalm when the "R" (*Response*) appears. (See instructions for singing the psalms, pages 20-25.) The response texts in this psalter come directly from the psalms, composite ideas from one or more psalm verses, other biblical passages, and fragments of familiar hymns. These responses highlight the meaning of the psalms and facilitate their use throughout the Christian year. See "Index of Psalms for Sundays and Special Days," pages 259-261.

The following texts illustrate the diverse traditions represented in the response texts (number in parenthesis indicates response number in Appendix A, pages 179-234):

(R 30)

> A mighty fortress is our God
> a bulwark never failing. (Martin Luther)

(R 9)

> Many and great, O God, are thy things,
> > Maker of earth and sky. (Native American Hymn)

(R 6)

> There is a balm in Gilead,
> > to make the wounded whole. (African American Spiritual)

The music of the responses is also drawn in large measure from hymnic traditions, for example:

(R 19) PASSION CHORALE

(R51) NUN DANKET

(R 62) YIGDAL

There are also composed and adapted musical settings of responses by Alan Luff, Timothy E. Kimbrough, Jane Marshall, Richard Proulx, Donald E. Saliers, Gary Alan Smith, and Carlton R. Young.

C. Inclusive Language

This psalter has been prepared for corporate worship and uses inclusive language for God, the assembly of the faithful, and humankind. The concerns for inclusive language are theological, sociological, and psychological, since the way we speak of God, others, and ourselves molds our faith, relationships, and personal lives. As the New Revised Standard Version illustrates, the language of the scriptures embodies a certain range of options for inclusive language.

1. Language for God

In the psalms there are primarily two names for deity—*YHWH* and *'Elohim*—"Lord" and "God" respectively. *YHWH* is the distinctive name of the God of the Hebrew scriptures, which was not pronounced, out of a sense of tremendous awe that surrounded the divine name and for fear of profaning it. The word 'Adonai was usually substituted for YHWH when the biblical text was read and is traditionally translated "Lord." The same translation appears when 'Adonai occurs in the biblical text. 'Adon, "Lord," is Israel's most characteristic way of referring to God. God's people perceived YHWH to be the Lord of creation, the world, all life, and as the Holy One who expects obedience from the faithful.

As in the New Revised Standard Version, YHWH is generally rendered "Lord" in this psalter. One cannot maintain on the basis of the biblical text *per se* that "Lord" is gender specific. The use of the word *lord* in English feudalism is most specific. If there were residual connotations of the term in colonial America, they are not a part of North American English-language usage, and Americans have never had an honorary title of "lord" nor a House of Lords. The social location of the name "Lord" in North America is primarily in the religious community as a form of address for deity and is therefore used in this psalter interchangeably with "God."

The other divine name, 'Elohim, is translated "God" and is a plural form of the name 'El, though it usually occurs with a singular verb. 'Elohim is a more general term for God than YHWH and could perhaps be rendered "deity."

Masculine pronouns (he, him, his) for God are rendered here by "Lord" and "God" (possessive forms: "Lord's," "God's," "of God," "of the Lord"), since they are used interchangeably, and occasionally a relative or demonstrative pronoun has been utilized. There is no strong evidence in the language of the scriptures that the biblical writers intended to convey divine masculinity by the use of masculine pronouns for God nor the opposite of femaleness, hence the use of the divine names "Lord" and "God," for which they are but substitutes. When the divine names are read corporately in place of pronouns, they often intensify the meaning, cogency, and dynamism of the psalms.

When the Hebrew word *melek* ("king") is used metaphorically in reference to God, it is translated "Ruler." When it refers to an earthly king, such as David, it is translated "king." Occasionally when *melek* refers to one who rules on God's behalf, "king" is also retained.

2. Generic References to Persons

The New Revised Standard Version renders generic references to persons in the plural. For example, Ps. 1:1*ab* is translated as follows:

> Blessed are *those*
> who do not walk in the counsel of the wicked.

The Hebrew word *ha'ish* ("the man") does not designate a specific "man" but is a generic reference to any person, hence the translation "those." Likewise, indefinite singular pronouns with generic reference are rendered by "they," "them," "themselves," or "their."

With the use of inclusive language, every attempt has been made not to change verbal structures nor the discourse of the original texts and to maintain the integrity of biblical language.

When we sing or say the psalms, we join with the faithful around the world and across denominational and religious boundaries in a song to the Creator. Indeed, the theology of the psalms forms the foundation of an ecumenical, doxological theology. The psalms bring us together in faith and belief, prayer and praise, worship and daily routine, despair and joy. They unite us as one voice in God's praise and self-examination. They allow us to be ourselves before God and others, and to respond in faithfulness!

> "O sing to the Lord a new song;
> sing to the Lord, all the earth!" (Ps. 96:1)

Reading and Singing *Psalms for Praise and Worship*

Psalms for Praise and Worship provides a blending of responsorial and antiphonal approaches to the public use of the psalms. The responsorial format of this psalter affords the following primary options for its reading and singing.

Reading *Psalms for Praise and Worship*

There are a number of possibilities for reading the psalms, ranging from unison reading to alternating groups of readers; for example:

1. Sections of a psalm or shorter psalms such as Psalm 133 may be read by the group in unison.

2. The psalm or psalm portions may be read in responsorial style as follows:

   a. The leader reads the light-face type and the congregation the bold type.
   b. The congregation is divided into two groups which alternate reading the light and bold-face type.

3. Responses ("R") may be used in responsorial style as follows:
   a. The leader reads the response.
   b. The congregation repeats the response.
   c. The psalm is read in a responsorial style as described above under 2.
   d. At the designation "R" the response is read together by leader and congregation. At the end of each paragraph at the designation "R" the response is read together by the leader and congregation.

The purchaser of this volume is granted permission to copy the appropriate response or responses for one-time use in a worship or educational setting provided the copyright notice and credits that appear with each selection are included.

Singing *Psalms for Praise and Worship*

The traditional psalm tone is the simplest form for singing the psalms. This psalter uses ten psalm tones (see pages 235-237), which may be selected for each psalm according to its mood; for example, bright or somber; and for the rhythm of the text. The leader will want to experiment with their use beyond those that have been suggested. For psalms which convey a bright and joyful mood Psalm Tones I, III, VI, VIII, and IX are suggested; for more somber and introspective texts Psalm Tones II, IV, V, VII, and X are suggested.

When introducing the singing of psalms with tones it is very important that the congregation experience the connection between speech and singing because this practice combines accentual English speech-rhythms with vocal performance. Introduce this style of singing by leading the group in reading a familiar psalm passage, such as Psalm 23:1-3, see below. As the people read, encourage them to accentuate, even exaggerate, the speech rhythms. Allow them to speak the text several times until they naturally begin to feel the ebb and flow, and the intrinsic accents within each phrase. Have them look away from the page and speak from memory. For many, this will be an entirely new and very satisfying aesthetic experience.

Then have them sing the note of recitation from memory, employing the same speech-rhythms, on a mid-pitch such as first space F. Sing in octaves, if there are both male and female voices. Let them glance at the page so that they begin to understand that occasionally the sung phrase will include both light and bold-face.

> The Lord is my shepherd; I sháll not want.
> **The Lord makes me lie down ín green pastures,**
> leads me besíde still waters,
> > restóres my life,
> **leads me ín right paths**
> > **for the sake of thé Lord's name.**   Psalm 23:1-3

After they have experienced the connection between speech and singing, you may begin to relate singing to the pointed text of the psalm, using the example from Psalm 46, below. A pointed text is one which has been marked with (´) to designate the shift of the voice from the note of recitation to the cadences.

Psalms for Praise and Worship includes both single and double chant-tones (see pages 235-237).

Single chant is comprised of two reciting tones for chanting the verses of the psalm. One or more syllables or words are sung on the reciting note until the point, (´) a diacritical mark, appears over the vowels á, é, í, ó, ú, or ý.

The point (´) at the beginning of a syllable or word indicates where the singers move from the reciting note |o| to the

half cadence notes ♪ ♪ ♩ |

or to the

ending cadence notes ♪ ♪ ♩ |

21

From the point (´) to the middle or end of recited text there are usually three syllables—one for each of the three notes in the half cadence or ending cadence. When there are more than three syllables, the additional syllables are usually sung to the last half note (as above for half-cadence). Occasionally a three-syllable word is sung to the two black notes by eliding the middle syllable; for example, "ev-e-ry" becomes "ev'ry," "of-fer-ing" becomes "off-ring," "mar-ve-lous" becomes "marv'lous." "Blessed" is sung "blest."

When there are only three words or syllables in a cadence, the first word or syllable is sung on the note of recitation, the second on the first two notes in the cadence, the third word or syllable on the ending note. For example, Psalm 104:35d would be sung this way:

When more syllables appear in a cadence than can be accommodated by the black notes, they should be sung by stressing the normal accent(s) of the word(s) and by adding more black notes (at the beginning of the cadence), or by singing the additional syllables on the final note (at the end). For example:

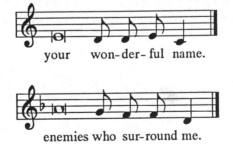

Single chant tones are structured as follows:

(1) a. the note of recitation |o| for chanting the text to the point (´)
    b. the half cadence of several tones;

(2) a. another note of recitation |o| for chanting the text
      to the point (´)
    b. the ending cadence of several tones.

In the following example, single chant tone 1 is used for singing Psalm 46. It is very important to lead your congregation's first experience with pointed chant by teaching this example by rote without reading from the page.

First, have the people speak in speech-rhythm *only* the text that is positioned under the note of recitation |o|; then sing it on a reciting tone. After they have sung it several times, add the half and ending cadences. Then have them open to the page so that they may see what they have just learned.

God is our refuge and strength, a very present help in trouble.

After they have sung the example several times, again without reading it, turn to Psalm 46, page 72, and very deliberately apply their experience one tone at a time, verse after verse, until they have sung the first paragraph, verses 1-7. *Do not move too quickly but allow them to move at their own speed.*

Sing the second paragraph of the psalm. Then sing the entire psalm adding the sung response No. 1 as shown below.

Double-chant tones can *only* be used in psalm passages where there are four, or groups of four, lines of pointed text between the responses. They are composed of two phrases of two reciting notes as in the following example using tone 6 for Psalm 46:

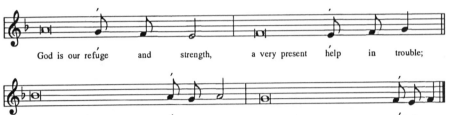

God is our refuge and strength, a very present help in trouble;

Therefore we will not fear though the earth should change, though the mountains shake in the heart of the sea.

Singing the Psalms and Responses:

The psalms and responses may be sung with or without accompaniment in a variety of ways:

1. The verses may be chanted by a soloist/cantor, choir, or congregation to one of the ten tones (see pages 235-237), and the responses (see pages 179-234) may be sung with the chanted verses. Pitch adjustments may need to be made when using a sung response with a psalm tone. See pages 237-243 for the transpositions of the Psalm Tones to higher or lower keys.

2. The verses may be chanted with the accompaniment included on pages 235-243. The responses may be accompanied either in octaves or with the harmony that is provided. Handbells may be used for intonations and may double the keyboard at the response. Guitar, Orff instruments, or additional keyboards may also be used.

3. The psalms may be sung in variants of 1 and 2; for example, the verses may be sung without accompaniment and the responses sung with accompaniment; or the verses may be sung in alternation by male and female soloists or choir alone, and the response sung by all.

4. Be sure to take sufficient time to properly introduce the congregation to new tones, responses, or when altering the performance practice.

Leading the Congregation in Psalm Singing:

The congregation should be directed from a lectern or music stand by a leader who is clearly visible and facing the congregation. The congregation may sing the psalms either standing or sitting. If a response is to be sung or read, it will need to be selected from pages 179-234 and either copied (see permission above) for one-time use or taught by rote at the beginning of the psalm.

a. The singing of the psalm is begun by the leader (soloist, cantor, choir), who receives the pitch from an instrument and sings the response (R).

b. The leader and congregation repeat the response.

c. The verses of the psalm are sung, as described above in 1-3.

d. At the designation R (response) printed within the psalm, the leader signals the congregation and, after receiving the pitch from an instrument, leads them in singing the response.

Combinations of Reading and Singing *Psalms for Praise and Worship*

Combining the reading and singing of psalms is particularly useful when the performance practice of psalm reading and singing is new to a congregation. When introducing combinations of reading or singing, it is important to remain flexible so as to avoid establishing one format as normative for all occasions. Performance directions should be explicitly stated and, in some instances, reviewed in a brief rehearsal.

There are two basic ways to combine reading and singing:

1. The psalm, or portions thereof, may be read in unison or responsorial styles (see above, page 19) by a leader or leaders, or by the congregation. The choir, soloist/cantor sings the response.

2. The psalm may be read in unison or responsorial styles by a leader or leaders, or by the congregation. Everyone sings the response.

PSALMS FOR PRAISE
AND WORSHIP

Psalm 1

R

1 Blessed are those
who do not walk in the counsel óf the wicked;
or stand in the way of sinners,
or sit in the séat of scoffers;
2 but their delight is in the law óf the Lord,
and on God's law they meditate dáy and night.
3 They are like trees
planted by stréams of water,
that yield their frúit in season,
and their leaves dó not wither.
In all that they dó, they prosper.   **R**

4 The wicked áre not so,
but are like chaff which the wind dríves away.
5 **Therefore the wicked will not stand ín the judgment;**
nor sinners in the congregation óf the righteous;
6 for the Lord knows the way óf the righteous,
but the way of the wickéd will perish.   **R**

Psalm 2

R

1 Why do the nations conspire,
and the people plót in vain?
2 The kings of the earth rise up,
and the rulers take counsel together
against God and God's anóinted, saying,
3 **"Let us búrst their bonds,**
and cast their córds from us."
4 The One who sits in the héavens laughs,
and holds them ín derision.
5 Then God will speak to them in anger,
and terrify them in fúry, saying,
6 **"I have set my king on Zion, my hóly hill."**   **R**

7 I will tell of the decree óf the Lord
who said to me: "You are my son,
today I have begótten you.
8 **Ask of me, and I will make the nations your héritage,**
and the ends of the earth yóur possession.
9 **You shall break them with a ród of iron,**
and dash them in pieces like a pótter's vessel."   **R**

¹⁰ Now, therefore, O kíngs, be wise;
  be warned, O rulers óf the earth.
¹¹ **Serve the Lord with féar and trembling;**
¹²   humble yourselves befóre the Lord
lest God be angry, and you perish in the way;
  for God's wrath is quíckly kindled.
Blessed are all who take refuge ín the Lord. **R**

Psalm 3

R

¹ O Lord, how many are my foes!
  Many are rising ágainst me;
² **many are saying of me,**
  "There is no help from God fór that one."
³ But you, O Lord, are a shíeld about me,
  my glory, and the lifter óf my head.
⁴ **I cry aloud tó the Lord**
  who answers me from God's hóly hill. **R**

⁵ I lie down and sleep;
  I wake again, for the Lórd sustains me.
⁶ **I am not afraid of ten thousand people**
  who have set themselves against me on évery side.
⁷ Aríse, O Lord!
  Deliver me, Ó my God!
For you strike all my enemies ón the cheek,
  you break the teeth óf the wicked.
⁸ **Deliverance belongs tó the Lord;**
  your blessing be upón your people! **R**

Psalm 4

R

¹ Answer me when I call, O God óf my right!
  You have given me room when I was in distress.
  Be gracious to me, and héar my prayer.
² How long, O people, shall my honor súffer shame?
  How long will you love emptiness, and seek áfter lies?
³ But know that the Lord has set apárt the faithful;
  The Lord hears whén I call. **R**

⁴ Be angry, but dó not sin;
  commune with your own hearts on your beds, ánd be silent.

5   Offer right sácrifices,
       and put your trust ín the Lord.
6   There are many who say, "O that we might sée some good!
       Lift up the light of your countenance upon ús, O Lord!"
7   You have put more joy ín my heart
       than have their gráin and wine.
8   **In peace I will both lie dówn and sleep,**
       for you alone, O Lord, make me lie dówn in safety.   **R**

Psalm 5

R

1   Hear my wórds, O Lord;
       give heed tó my groaning.
2   **Harken to the sound óf my cry,**
       my Ruler and my God,
       for to yóu I pray.
3   O Lord, in the morning you héar my voice;
       in the morning I prepare a sacrifice for yóu, and watch.
4   **For you are not a God who delights in wíckedness;**
       evil may not dwéll with you.
5   The boastful may not stand befóre your eyes;
       you hate all évildoers.
6   **You destroy those whó speak lies;**
       the Lord abhors the bloodthirsty ánd deceitful.
7   But I, through the abundance of your stéadfast love,
       will énter your house.
       Toward your hóly temple
       I will worship yóu in awe.   **R**

8   Lead me, O Lord, in your righteousness
       because of my énemies;
       make your way stráight before me.
9   For there is no truth ín their mouth;
       their heart ís destruction,
       their throat is an ópen grave,
       they flatter wíth their tongue.
10 Make them bear their gúilt, O God;
       let them fall by théir own counsels;
       because of their many transgressions cást them out,
       for they have rebélled against you.
11 Let all who take refuge in you be glad,
       let them ever síng for joy;
       defend them, that those who love your name may tríumph in you.

31

12   For you bless the ríghteous, O Lord;
      you cover them with favor ás a shield.   **R**

Psalm 6

R

1   O Lord, do not rebuke me ín your anger,
      nor chasten me ín your wrath.
2   **Be gracious to me, O Lord, fór I languish;**
      O Lord, heal me, for my bones are stricken.
3   **My whole being also is stricken with terror.**
      But you, O Lórd—how long?   **R**

4   Turn, O Lord, sáve my life;
      deliver me for the sake of your stéadfast love.
5   **For in death there is no remémbrance of you;**
      in Sheol who can gíve you praise?
6   I am weary wíth my moaning;
      every night I flood my bed with tears;
      I drench my couch wíth my weeping.
7   **My eye wastes away becáuse of grief,**
      it grows weak because of áll my foes.   **R**

  Depart from me, all you wórkers of evil,
      for the Lord has heard the sound óf my weeping.
  The Lord has heard my súpplication;
      the Lord accépts my prayer.
  All my enemies shall be ashamed and strícken with terror;
      they shall turn back, and be put to shame ín a moment.   **R**

Psalm 7

R

1   O Lord my God, in you Í take refuge;
      save me from all my pursuers, and delíver me,
2   or like a lion they will tear mé apart;
      they will drag me away, with no óne to rescue.
3   **O Lord my God, if I have done this,**
      if there is wrong ín my hands,
4   **if I have repaid my ally with harm**
      or plundered my foe wíthout cause,
5   then let the enemy pursue and óvertake me,
      trample my life to the ground,
      and lay my soul ín the dust.

6 Rise up, O Lord, ín your anger,
     rise up against the fury of my enemies;
     awake, O my God; you have appóinted a judgment.
7 Let the assembly of the peoples be gáthered about you;
     and over it take your séat on high.
8 The Lord judges the peoples;
     judge me, O Lord, according to my ríghteousness
     and according to the integrity that ís in me.   **R**

9 O righteous God,
     who tries the mínds and hearts,
   let the evil of the wicked come to an end,
     but estáblish the righteous.
10 God is my shield,
     who saves the upríght in heart.
11 God is a righteous judge,
     and a severe God évery day.
12 If one does not repent, God will shárpen a sword;
     God has bent and strúng a bow;
13 God has prepared déadly weapons,
     making arrows fíery shafts.   **R**

14 See how they concéive evil,
     and are pregnant with mischief,
     and bríng forth lies.
15 They make a pit, dígging it out,
     and fall into the hole that théy have made.
16 Their mischief returns upon théir own heads;
     their violence descends upon their ówn foreheads.
17 I will give thanks for the righteousness óf the Lord.
     I will sing praises to the name of the Lord, thé most High. **R**

Psalm 8

R

1 O Lórd, our Lord,
     how majestic is your name in áll the earth!
2 Your glory is chanted abóve the heavens
     by the mouth of bábes and infants;
   you have set up a defense agáinst your foes,
     to still the enemy and thé avenger.   **R**

3 When I look at your heavens, the work óf your fingers,
     the moon and the stars which you háve established;
4 what are human beings that you are míndful of them,
     and mortals, that you cáre for them?

5 Yet you have made them little léss than God,
   and crowned them with glóry and honor.
6 You have given them dominion over the works óf your hands;
   you have put all things únder their feet,
7 all sheep and oxen,
   and also the beasts óf the field,
8 the birds of the air, and the fish of the sea,
   whatever passes along the paths óf the seas.
9 **O Lórd, our Lord,**
   how majestic is your name in áll the earth!　　**R**

Psalm 9

R

1 I will gives thanks to the Lord with mý whole heart;
   I will tell of all of your wónderful deeds.
2 **I will be glad and rejóice in you,**
   I will sing praise to your name, Ó Most High.
3 When my enemies turned back,
   they stumbled and pérished before you.
4 For you have maintained mý just cause;
   you have sat on the throne giving ríghteous judgment.
5 **You have rebuked the nations, you have destróyed the wicked;**
   you have blotted out their name foréver and ever.
6 **The enemy have vanished in everlásting ruins;**
   you have uprooted their cities;
   the very memory of thém has perished.
7 But the Lord sits enthróned forever,
   and has established a thróne for judgment;
8 **The Lord judges the world with ríghteousness,**
   judges the peoples with équity.
9 The Lord is a stronghold for thé oppressed,
   a stronghold in tímes of trouble.
10 **And those who know your name put their trúst in you,**
   for you, O Lord, have not forsaken thóse who seek you.　　**R**

11 Sing praises to the Lord, who dwélls in Zion!
   Tell God's deeds amóng the peoples!
12 For the Lord who avenges blood remémbers them;
   and does not forget the cry of thé afflicted.
13 **Be gracious to mé, O Lord!**
   See what I suffer from thóse who hate me;
14 **You are the One who delivers me from the gates of death,**
   that I may recount áll your praises,

that, in the gates of daughter Zion,
 I may rejoice in your delíverance.   **R**

15 The nations have sunk in the pit whích they made;
 their own foot has been caught in the net whích they hid.
16 The Lord is made known! The Lord has execúted judgment!
 The wicked are snared in the work of théir own hands.
17 The wicked shall depárt to Sheol,
 all the nations that forgót God.
18 **For the needy shall not always bé forgotten,**
 and the hope of the poor shall not pérish forever.
19 Arise, O Lord! Let no óne prevail;
 let the nations be júdged before you!
20 Put them in féar, O Lord!
 Let the nations know that they are ónly mortal!   **R**

Psalm 10

R

1 Why do you stand far óff, O Lord?
 Why do you hide yourself in tímes of trouble?
2 **In arrogance the wicked persecúte the poor;**
 let them be caught in the schemes they háve devised.
3 For the wicked boast of their ówn desires,
 the greedy curse and renóunce the Lord.
4 **In the pride of their countenance the wicked say, "God will not**
 séek it out;"
 all their thoughts are: "There ís no God."
5 Their ways prosper át all times.
 Your judgments are on high, out of their sight;
 as for their foes, they snéer at them.
6 **They say to themselves, "I shall nót be moved;**
 throughout all generations I shall not meet advérsity."   **R**

7 Their mouths are filled with cursing, deceit and víolence;
 mischief and wrong are únder their tongue.
8 They sit in ambush in the víllages;
 they murder the innocent from híding places.
9 **Their eyes stealthily watch fór the helpless,**
 they lurk in secret like a lion ín its den;
 they lurk that they may séize the poor;
 they seize the poor when they draw them intó their net.
10 They stoop, they crouch,
 and the helpless fall bý their might.
11 **They think in their heart, "God has forgotten,**
 God has turned away and will néver see it."   **R**

¹² Arise, O Lord; O God, lift úp your hand;
  do not forget thé afflicted.
¹³ **Why do the wicked renóunce God,**
  and say in their hearts, "You will not call tó account"?
¹⁴ But you see; indeed you note trouble ánd vexation,
  that you may take it intó your hands;
  the helpless commit themsélves to you;
  you have been the helper óf the orphan.   R

¹⁵ Break the arm of the wicked and évildoers;
  seek out their wickedness until yóu find none.
¹⁶ The Lord is Ruler forevér and ever;
  the nations shall perish fróm God's land.
¹⁷ O Lord, you will hear the desire óf the meek;
  you will stréngthen their heart,
  you will respond
¹⁸ **by doing justice for the orphan and thé oppressed,**
  so that people on earth may create térror no more.   R

Psalm 11

R

¹ In the Lord Í take refuge.
  How can you sáy to me,
  "Flee like a bird to the mountains;
² See how the wicked bénd the bow,
  they have fitted their arrow to the string,
  to shoot in the dark at the úpright in heart.
³ **If the foundations áre destroyed,**
  what can the ríghteous do?"
⁴ The Lord whose throne is in heaven,
  sees and exámines all mortals.
⁵ **The Lord tests the righteous and the wicked,**
  and hates the lover of víolence.
⁶ The Lord will rain coals of fire and sulphur ón the wicked;
  a scorching wind shall be the portion óf their cup.
⁷ **For the Lord is righteous**
  and loves ríghteous deeds;
  the upright shall behold the face óf the Lord.   R

Psalm 12

R

¹ Help, O Lord; no one who is gódly is left,
  for the faithful have vanished from húmankind.

36

2 They utter lies tó each other;
    they speak with flattering lips and a dóuble heart.
3 **May the Lord cut off all fláttering lips,**
    the tongue that mákes great boasts,
4 **those who say, "With our tongues we wíll prevail,**
    our lips are our own; who ís our master?"
5 The Lord says, "Now I will arise,
    because the póor are plundered,
    because the needy groan;
    I will place them in the safety for whích they long."
6 **The promises of the Lord are promises thát are pure,**
    silver refined in an earthen furnace,
    purified séven times.
7 Protect us, O Lord;
    guard us from this generátion forever.
8 **The wicked prowl on every side**
    when vileness is exalted among húmankind.   **R**

Psalm 13

R

1 How long, O Lord? Will you forget mé forever?
    How long will you hide your fáce from me?
2 How long must I bear pain in my soul,
    and have sorrow in my heart áll the day?
    How long shall my enemy be exalted óver me?   **R**

3 Consider and answer me, O Lórd my God;
    lighten my eyes, lest I sleep the sléep of death;
4 lest my enemy say, "I háve prevailed; "
    lest my foes rejoice because Í am shaken.
5 But I trusted in your stéadfast love;
    my heart shall rejoice in yóur salvation.
6 I will sing tó the Lord,
    for the Lord has dealt ríchly with me.   **R**

Psalm 14

R

1 Fools say in their hearts, "There ís no God."
    They are corrupt, they do abominable deeds,
    there is none thát does good.
2 The Lord looks down from heaven ón all people,

to see if there are any that are wise,
who seek áfter God.
3   **They have all gone astray, they are all alíke perverse;**
there is none that does good,
nó, not one.   R

4   Have they no knowledge, the evildoers
who eat up my people as théy eat bread,
and do not call upón the Lord?
5   **There they shall be ín great terror,**
for God is with the generation óf the righteous.
6   You would confound the plans óf the poor,
but the Lord ís their refuge.
7   **O that deliverance for Israel would cóme from Zion!**
When the Lord restores their fortunes,
Jacob shall rejoice and Israel sháll be glad!"   R

Psalm 15

R

1   O Lord, who shall dwell ín your tent?
Who shall dwell on your hóly hill?
2   **The one who walks blamelessly, and does whát is right,**
and speaks truth fróm the heart;
3   who does not slander with the tongue,
and does no evil tó a friend,
nor takes up a reproach agáinst a neighbor;
4   **in whose eyes a reproach ís despised,**
but who honors those who féar the Lord;
5   who does not loan money at interest,
and does not take a bribe against the ínnocent.
Whoever does these things shall néver be moved.   R

Psalm 16

R

1   Preserve me, O God, for in you Í take refuge.
2   **I say to the Lord, "O Lord, you are my fortune,**
ónly you!"
3   As for the holy ones ín the land,
and the mighty ones in whom was all mý delight,
4   let their pain increase and their lúst persist!
I will not pour out their libations of blood
or take their names upón my lips.   R

⁵ The Lord is my chosen portion and my cup;
   you hóld my lot.
⁶ **The boundary lines have fallen for me in pleasant places;**
   I have a goodly héritage.
⁷ I bless the Lord who gíves me counsel;
   my heart also instructs me ín the night.
⁸ **I have set the Lord álways before me;**
   the Lord is at my right hand;
   I shall nót be moved.   R

⁹ Therefore my heart is glad, and my sóul rejoices;
   my body also dwélls secure.
¹⁰ **For you do not give me úp to Sheol,**
   or let your godly one sée the Pit.
¹¹ You show me the páth of life;
   in your presence there is fullness of joy,
   in your right hand are pleasures for évermore.   R

Psalm 17

R

¹ Hear a just cause, O Lord; attend tó my cry!
   Hear my prayer from lips free óf deceit!
² From you let my vindicátion come!
   Let your eyes sée the right!
³ If you try my heart, if you visit mé by night,
   if you test me, you will find no wickedness in me;
   my mouth does nót transgress.
⁴ Concerning what óthers do,
   I have avoided the ways of the violent by fóllowing your word.
⁵ **My steps have held fast tó your paths,**
   my feet háve not slipped.   R

⁶ I call upon you, for you will answer mé, O God;
   listen to me, héar my words.
⁷ **Wondrously show your stéadfast love,**
   O savior of those who seek refuge
   from their adversaries at yóur right hand.   R

⁸ Guard me as the apple óf the eye;
   hide me in the shadow óf your wings,
⁹ **from the wicked whó attack me,**
   my deadly enemies whó surround me.

10 They close their héarts to pity;
        with their mouths they speak árrogantly.
11 **They track me down; now théy surround me;**
        they set their eyes to cast me tó the ground.
12 They are like a lion éager for prey,
        as a young lion lurking ín ambush.
13 **Arise, O Lord! confront them, óverthrow them!**
        By your sword deliver my life fróm the wicked,
14 **by your hánd, O Lord,**
        from mortals whose life's portion is ín the world.
    May their belly be filled with the emptiness
        you have stóred for them;
        may their children be glutted with it;
        may they leave some of it for their líttle ones.
15 **As for me, I shall behold your face in ríghteousness;**
        when I awake I shall be satisfied, behólding your
        presence.   R

Psalm 18

R

1 I love you, O Lórd, my strength.
2 **The Lord is my rock, my fortress, my delíverer,**
        my God, my rock in whom Í take refuge,
        my shield, and the horn of my salvation, mý stronghold.
3 **I call upon the Lord, who is worthy tó be praised,**
        and I shall be saved from my énemies.
4 The cords of death encómpassed me,
        the torrents of perdition assailed me;
5 the cords of Sheol entangled me,
        the snares of death confrónted me.
6 **In my distress I called upón the Lord;**
        to my God I críed for help.
    From the temple the Lord héard my voice,
        and my cry réached God's ears.   R

7 Then the earth réeled and rocked;
        the foundations of the mountains trembled
        and quaked because Gód was angry.
8 **Smoke went up from God's nostrils,**
        devouring fire fróm God's mouth,
        glowing cóals flamed forth.
9 God bowed the heavens, ánd came down;
        thick darkness was únder God's feet.
10 **God rode on a chérub and flew,**
        and came swiftly upon the wings óf the wind.

11 God made darkness a surróunding veil,
    thick clouds dark with water a cánopy.

12 **Out of the brightness befóre God**
    hailstones and coals of fire
    broke thróugh the clouds.

13 The Lord thundered ín the heavens,
    and the Most High spoke hailstones and cóals of fire.

14 The Lord sent out arrows, and scáttered them,
    flashed lightning and róuted them.

15 **Then the channels of the séa were seen,**
    and the foundations of the earth wére laid bare
    at your rebúke, O Lord,
    at the fierce breath óf your nostrils.   **R**

16 The Lord reached down from on high ánd took me,
    drew me out of míghty waters,

17 delivered me from my strong énemy,
    from those who hated me;
    for they were too stróng for me.

18 **They confronted me in the day of my calámity;**
    but the Lord was mý support

19   **brought me forth into á broad place,**
    and delivered me, because the Lord delíghted in me.   **R**

20 The Lord rewarded me according to my ríghteousness;
    recompensed me according to the cleanness óf my hands.

21 **For I have kept the ways óf the Lord,**
    and have not transgressed agáinst my God.

22 For all God's ordinances áre before me,
    and God's statutes I did not put awáy from me.

23 **I was blameless befóre God**
    and I kept mysélf from guilt.

24 Therefore the Lord has recompensed me according to my
    ríghteousness,
    according to the cleanness of my hands ín God's sight.

25 **With the loyal you show yourself loyal;**
    with the blameless you show yóurself blameless;

26 **with the pure you show yourself pure;**
    and with the crooked you show yóurself crooked.

27 For you deliver a húmble people,
    but you bring down the háughty eyes.

28 **For you light my lámp, O Lord;**
    my God lights úp my darkness.

29 With you I can run ás a warrior,
    and with my God I can leap óver a wall.

30 **The way of Gód is perfect;**
    the word of the Lord is tested;
    it is a shield for all who take refuge ín the Lord.   **R**

31 For who is God excépt the Lord?
    And who is a rock besídes our God?—
32 **the God who girded mé with strength,**
    made mý way safe,
33 **made my feet líke the deer's,**
    and set me secure ón the heights.
34 God trains my hánds for war,
    so that my arms can bend a bów of bronze.
35 **You have given me the shield of yóur salvation,**
    and your right hand supported me;
    your help has máde me great.
36 You gave me a wide place for my steps únder me,
    and my feet díd not slip.
37 **I pursued my enemies and óvertook them;**
    and did not turn back until they wére consumed.
38 I struck them down, so that they were not áble to rise;
    they fell únder my feet.
39 **For you girded me with strength fór the battle;**
    you made my assailants sink únder me.   **R**

40 You made my enemies turn their bácks to me,
    and those who hated me Í destroyed.
41 They cried for help, but there was nóne to save;
    they cried to the Lord, who did not ánswer them.
42 I pulverized them like the dirt befóre the wind;
    I cast them out like the mire óf the streets.
43 **You delivered me from strife wíth the peoples;**
    you made me head of the nations;
    people whom I had not knówn served me.
44 **As soon as they heard of me they obeyed me;**
    foreigners came crínging to me.
45 **Foreigners lost heart,**
    and came trembling out of théir strongholds.   **R**

46 The Lord lives! Blessed bé my rock!
    Exalted be the God of mý salvation,
47 the God who gáve me vengeance
    and subdued peoples únder me;
48 who delivered me fróm my enemies;
    indeed, you exalted me above my adversaries;
    you delivered me fróm the violent.

49 For this I will extol you, O Lord, amóng the nations;
   and sing praises tó your name.
50 God gives great triumphs tó the king,
   and shows steadfast love to the anointed,
   to David and his descéndants forever.   **R**

Psalm 19

R

1 The heavens are telling the glóry of God;
   and the firmament proclaims God's hándiwork.
2 **Day to day póurs forth speech,**
   and night to night decláres knowledge.
3 There is no speech, nor áre there words;
   their voice ís not heard;
4 **yet their voice goes out through áll the earth,**
   and their words to the end óf the world.
   In them God has set a tent fór the sun,
5 which comes forth like a bridegroom leaving his chamber,
   and runs its course with joy like á strong man.
6 **Its rising is from the end of the heavens,**
   and its circuit to the énd of them,
   and nothing is hid fróm its heat.   **R**

7 The law of the Lórd is perfect,
   revíving the soul;
   the testimony of the Lórd is sure,
   making wíse the simple;
8 the precepts of the Lórd are right,
   rejóicing the heart;
   the commandment of the Lórd is pure,
   enlíghtening the eyes;
9 the fear of the Lórd is clean,
   endúring forever;
   the ordinances of the Lórd are true
   and righteous áltogether.
10 More to be desired are théy than gold,
   even múch fine gold;
   sweeter álso than honey
   and drippings of the hóneycomb.   **R**

11 Moreover by them is your sérvant warned;
   in keeping them there is gréat reward.
12 **But who can understánd one's errors?**
   Clear me from hídden faults.

43

13 Also keep back your servant from the ínsolent;
 let them not have dominion óver me!
Then I sháll be blameless,
 and innocent of gréat transgression.
14 **Let the words of my mouth and the meditation of my heart**
 be acceptable ín your sight,
 O Lord, my rock and mý redeemer.   R

Psalm 20

R

1 May the Lord answer you in the dáy of trouble!
 The name of the God of Jácob protect you!
2 May the Lord send you help from the sánctuary,
 and give you suppórt from Zion!
3 **May the Lord remember all your ófferings,**
 and accept your burnt sácrifices!
4 May the Lord grant you your héart's desire,
 and fulfill áll your plans!
5 **May we shout for joy over your victory,**
 and in the name of our God set úp our banners!
May the Lord fulfill all yóur petitions!   R

6 Now I know that the Lord will deliver and answer God's anointed one
 from hóly heaven
 with mighty victories by the Lórd's right hand.
7 **Some boast of cháriots and horses;**
 we boast of the name óf the Lord.
8 They will collápse and fall;
 but we shall rise and stánd upright.
9 Give victory to the mónarch, O Lord;
 answer us whén we call.   R

Psalm 21

R

1 The king rejoices in your stréngth, O Lord;
 how greatly he exults ín your help!
2 You have given him his héart's desire,
 and have not withheld the request óf his lips.
3 For you meet him wíth rich blessings;
 you set a crown of fine gold ón his head.
4 He asked you for life; you gáve it to him,
 length of days foréver and ever.

44

5   His glory is great thróugh your help;
     you bestow majesty and spléndor on him.

6   You bestow on him bléssings forever;
     you make him glad with the joy óf your presence.

7   For the king trusts ín the Lord;
     and through the steadfast love of the Most High he shall
      nót be moved.   R

8   Your hand will find out all your énemies;
     your right hand will find out thóse who hate you.

9   You will make them like a fiery furnace
     when yóu appear.
   The Lord will swallow them up in wrath;
     and fire wíll consume them.

10 You will destroy their offspring fróm the earth,
     and their children from among húmankind.

11 **If they plan evil against you,**
     if they devise mischief, they will nót succeed.

12 For you will put them to flight;
     you will aim at their faces wíth your bows.

13 **Be exalted, O Lord, ín your strength!**
     We will sing and práise your power.   R

Psalm 22

R

1   My God, my God, why have you forsáken me?
     Why are you so far from helping me, from the words óf my
      groaning?

2   O my God, I cry by day, but you dó not answer;
     and by night, but fínd no rest.

3   Yet you, the praise of Israel,
     are enthroned in hóliness.

4   **In you our forebears trusted;**
     they trusted, and you delívered them.

5   To you they cried, ánd were saved;
     in you they trusted, and were not dísappointed.   R

6   But I am a wórm, not human;
     scorned by others, and despised bý the people.

7   **All who see me móck at me,**
     they make mouths at me, they wag their héads and say:

8   "You committed your cause tó the Lord;
     let the Lord delíver you.
     Let the Lord réscue you,
     for the Lord delíghts in you!"

9 Yet it was you, O God, who took me fróm the womb;
    you kept me safe on my móther's breast.
10 On you I was cast fróm my birth,
    and since my mother bore me, you have béen my God.
11 **Be not fár from me,**
    for trouble is near
    and there is no óne to help.   **R**

12 Many bulls encírcle me,
    strong bulls of Bashan surróund me;
13 they open wide their móuths at me,
    like a ravening and róaring lion.
14 I am poured óut like water,
    and all my bones are óut of joint;
    my heart ís like wax,
      melted withín my breast;
15 my mouth is dried up like a potsherd,
    and my tongue sticks tó my jaws;
      you lay me in the dúst of death.
16 Indeed, dogs súrround me;
    a company of evildoers encircles me;
    my hands and féet are bound;
17 I can count áll my bones;
    they stare and gloat óver me;
18 they divide my gárments among them,
    and cast lots fór my clothing.   **R**

19 But you, O Lord, be not fár away!
    O my help, hasten tó my aid!
20 **Deliver my soul fróm the sword,**
    my life from the power óf the dog!
21 Save me from the mouth óf the lion!
    From the horns of the wild oxen you have réscued me.
22 **I will tell of your name tó my kindred;**
    in the midst of the congregation Í will praise you;
23 All who fear the Lórd, shout praise!
    All you offspring of Jacob, glorify God!
    Stand in awe, all you offspring of Ísrael!
24 **For God did not despise or abhor**
    the affliction of thé afflicted,
    nor hide from me,
    but heard when Í cried out.   **R**

25 From you comes my praise in the great cóngregation;
    my vows I will pay before those who wórship the Lord.
26 The poor shall eat and be sátisfied;
    those who seek the Lord shall praise the Lord!
    May your hearts líve forever!
27 All the ends of the earth shall remember
    and turn tó the Lord;
    and all the families of the nations
      shall worship befóre the Lord.
28 For dominion belongs to the Lord,
    who rules óver the nations.
29 **All who are prosperous in the land**
    shall eat and bow down tó the Lord.
    All who go down to the dust shall bow befóre the Lord,
      for they cannot keep themsélves alive.
30 **Posterity shall sérve the Lord;**
    each generation shall téll of the Lord,
31 and proclaim deliverance to a people yét unborn:
    surely the Lórd has done it.   **R**

Psalm 23

R

1 The Lord is my shepherd, I sháll not want;
2   **The Lord makes me lie down ín green pastures,**
    leads me besíde still waters;
3   restóres my life,
    leads me ín right paths
      for the sake of thé Lord's name.
4 Even though I walk through the darkest valley,
    I féar no evil;
    for you are with me;
      your rod and your staff,
      they cómfort me.   **R**

5 You prepare a table before me
    in the presence of my énemies;
    you anoint my head with oil,
      my cup óverflows.
6 Only goodness and mercy shall follow me
    all the days óf my life;
    and I shall dwell in the house of the Lord
      as long ás I live.   **R**

Psalm 24

R

1 The earth is the Lord's and the fúllness thereof,
  the world and those who dwéll therein;
2 for God has founded it upón the seas,
  and established it upón the rivers.
3 Who shall ascend the hill óf the Lord?
  And who shall stand in God's hóly place?
4 **Those who have clean hands ánd pure hearts,**
  who do not set their minds on falsehood,
  and do not swear decéitfully.
5 They will receive blessing fróm the Lord,
  and vindication from the God of théir salvation.
6 Such is the generation of those who séek the Lord,
  who seek the face of the Gód of Jacob.   R

7 Lift up your heads, O gates!
  and be lifted up, O áncient doors!
  that the Ruler of glory máy come in.
8 **Who is the Rúler of glory?**
  The Lord, strong and mighty,
  The Lord, míghty in battle!
9 **Lift up your héads, O gates!**
  and be lifted up, O ancient doors!
  that the Ruler of glory máy come in.
10 Who is this Rúler of glory?
   The Lord of hosts,
   the Lord is the Rúler of glory!   R

Psalm 25

R

1 To you, O Lord, I lift úp my soul.
2 **O my God, in yóu I trust,**
  let me not be pút to shame;
  let not my enemies triumph óver me.
3 Let none that wait for you be pút to shame;
  let them be ashamed who are clothed with tréachery.
4 Make me to know your wáys, O Lord;
  teach mé your paths.
5 Lead me in your truth, ánd teach me,
  for you are the God of my salvation;
  for you I wait áll day long.   R

⁶ Be mindful of your mercy, O Lord, and of your stéadfast love,
for they have been fróm of old.

⁷ **Do not remember the sins of my youth, or mý transgressions;**
according to your steadfast love remember me,
for the sake of your góodness, O Lord!

⁸ Good and upright ís the Lord;
therefore the Lord instructs sinners ín the way,

⁹ leads the humble in whát is right,
and teaches thém their way.

¹⁰ **All the paths of the Lord are steadfast love and fáithfulness,**
for those who keep the Lord's covenant and téstimonies.   **R**

¹¹ For your name's sáke, O Lord,
pardon my guilt, for ít is great.

¹² **Who are they that féar the Lord?**
God will teach them the way that théy should choose.

¹³ They will abide in prospérity,
and their children shall posséss the land.

¹⁴ **The friendship of the Lord is for those whó are faithful;**
God makes known to them the cóvenant.

¹⁵ My eyes are ever tóward the Lord,
who will pluck my feet out óf the net.

¹⁶ **Turn to me, and be grácious to me;**
for I am lonely ánd afflicted.

¹⁷ Relieve the troubles óf my heart,
and bring me out of mý distresses.

¹⁸ **Consider my affliction ánd my trouble,**
and forgive áll my sins.   R

¹⁹ Consider how many áre my foes,
and with what violent hatréd they hate me.

²⁰ **O guard my life, and delíver me;**
let me not be put to shame, for I take réfuge in you.

²¹ May integrity and uprightness preserve me,
for I wáit for you.

²² **Redeem Israel, O God,**
out of áll its troubles.   R

Psalm 26

R

¹ Vindicate mé, O Lord,
for I have walked in my integrity,
and I have trusted in the Lord without wávering.

² **Prove me, O Lórd, and try me;**
test my héart and mind.

3   For your steadfast love is befóre my eyes,
        and I walk in your fáithfulness.
4   **I do not sít with liars,**
        nor do I consort with hýpocrites;
5   I hate the company of évildoers,
        and I will not sit wíth the wicked.
6   **I wash my hands in ínnocence,**
        and go around your áltar, O Lord,
7   **singing aloud a song óf thanksgiving,**
        and telling all your wóndrous deeds.   **R**

8   O Lord, I love the house in whích you dwell,
        and the place where your glóry abides.
9   **Do not sweep me awáy with sinners,**
        nor my life with the blóodthirsty
10   **in whose hands are évil devices,**
        and whose right hands are fúll of bribes.
11   But as for me, I walk with intégrity;
        redeem me, and be grácious to me.
12   **My feet stand on lével ground;**
        in the great congregation I will bléss the Lord.   **R**

Psalm 27

R

1   The Lord is my light and mý salvation;
        whom sháll I fear?
        The Lord is the strength óf my life;
        of whom shall I bé afraid?
2   When evildoers assail me,
        to devóur my flesh,
    my adversaries and foes
        shall stúmble and fall.
3   **Though a host encamp against me,**
        my heart sháll not fear;
    though war arise against me,
        yet I will be cónfident.
4   One thing I asked óf the Lord,
        that will Í seek after;
    that I may dwell in the house óf the Lord
        all the days óf my life,
    to behold the beauty óf the Lord,
        and to inquire in thé Lord's temple.   **R**

5   The Lord will hide me in a shelter,
        in the dáy of trouble;
    will conceal me under the cover of a tent,
        and will set me high upón a rock.

6   **Now my head is lífted up**
        above my enemies róund about me;
    and I will offer sacrifices in the Lord's tent
        with shóuts of joy;
    I will sing and make melody tó the Lord.   **R**

7   Hear, O Lord, when I crý aloud,
        be gracious to me and ánswer me!

8   **"Come," my heart says, "seek thé Lord's face."**
        Your face, Lord, dó I seek.

9   Do not hide your fáce from me.
        Do not turn your servant away in anger,
        you who have béen my help.

10   **Do not cast me off, do not forsake me,**
        O God of mý salvation!
    If my father and mother forsake me,
        the Lord will táke me up.   **R**

11   Teach me your wáy, O Lord;
        and lead me on a level path
        because of my énemies.

12   **Do not give me up to the will of my ádversaries;**
        for false witnesses have risen against me,
        and they breathe out víolence.

13   I believe that I shall see the goodness óf the Lord
        in the land óf the living!

14   **Wait for the Lord;**
        be strong, and let your héart take courage.
    Wait fór the Lord!   **R**

Psalm 28

R

1   To you, O Lórd, I call;
        my rock, do not be déaf to me;
    if you are sílent to me,
        I become like those who go down tó the pit.

2   **Hear the voice of my supplication,**
        as I cry to yóu for help,
        as I lift up my hands
        toward your most holy sánctuary.   **R**

3   Take me not away wíth the wicked,
        with those who are wórkers of evil,
    who speak peace wíth their neighbors
        while mischief is ín their hearts.
4   **Repay them according to their work,**
        and according to the evil óf their deeds;
        repay them according to the work of their hands;
        render them their dúe reward.
5   **The Lord will break them down and build them úp no more,**
        because they do not regard the deeds of the Lord,
        or the work of thé Lord's hands.   R

6   Blessed be the Lord,
        who has heard the voice of my súpplications!
7   **The Lord is my strength and shield**
        in whom mý heart trusts;
        so I am helped, and my héart rejoices,
        and with my song I give thanks tó the Lord.
8   The Lord is the strength óf the people,
        the saving refuge of Gód's anointed.
9   **O save your people, and bléss your heritage;**
        be their shepherd, and carry thém forever.   R

Psalm 29

R

1   Ascribe to the Lord, O héavenly beings,
        ascribe to the Lord glóry and strength.
2   **Ascribe to the Lord a glórious name;**
        worship the Lord in hóly splendor.
3   The voice of the Lord is upón the waters;
        the God of glory thunders,
        the Lord, upon mány waters.
4   **The voice of the Lord is pówerful,**
        The voice of the Lord is full of májesty.   R

5   The voice of the Lord bréaks the cedars,
        the Lord breaks the cedars of Lébanon.
6   The Lord makes Lebanon to skip líke a calf,
        and Sirion like a yóung wild ox.
7   **The voice of the Lord flashes forth flámes of fire.**
8   The voice of the Lord shakes the wilderness,
        shakes the wílderness of Kadesh.
9   The voice of the Lord makes the oaks to whirl,
        and strips the fórests bare;
        and in God's temple áll cry, "Glory!"

10 The Lord sits enthroned óver the flood;
        the Lord sits enthroned as Rúler forever.
11 **May the Lord give strength tó God's people!**
    May the Lord bless the péople with peace!   **R**

Psalm 30

R

1 I will extol you, O Lord, for you have lífted me up,
        and did not let my foes rejoice óver me.
2 **O Lord my God, I cried to yóu for help,**
    and yóu healed me.
3 O Lord, you brought up my sóul from Sheol,
        restored me to life from among those gone down tó the pit. R

4 Sing praises to the Lord, Ó you saints,
        and give thanks to God's hóly name.
5 **Surely the Lord's anger is but fór a moment;**
    the Lord's favor is fór a lifetime.
    Weeping may tarry for the night
        but joy comes wíth the morning.
6 **As for me, I said in my prospérity,**
    "I shall néver be moved."
7 By your favor, O Lord,
        you had established me as á strong mountain;
    you hid your face,
        I wás dismayed.   R

8 To you, O Lórd, I cried,
        and to the Lord I made súpplication:
9 **"What profit is there in my death,**
    if I go down tó the pit?
    Will the dust praise you?
        Will it tell of your fáithfulness?
10 **Hear, O Lord, and be gracious to me!**
    O Lord, bé my helper!"
11 You have turned my mourning ínto dancing;
        you have loosed my sackcloth
        and girded mé with gladness,
12 that I may sing "glory" to you and nót be silent.
    O Lord, my God, I will give thanks to yóu forever.   R

Psalm 31

R

1 In you, O Lord, Í seek refuge;
    let me never be put to shame;
    in your righteousness, delíver me!
2 **Listen to me,**
    rescue me spéedily!
 Be a rock of refuge for me,
    a strong fortress to sáve me!
3 You are indeed my rock ánd my fortress;
    for your name's sake lead mé and guide me,
4 **take me out of the net which is hídden for me,**
    for you áre my refuge.
5 Into your hand I commít my spirit;
    you have redeemed me, O Lord, fáithful God.
6 **I hate those who pay regard tó vain idols;**
    but I trust ín the Lord.
7 I will rejoice and be glad in your stéadfast love,
    because you have seen my affliction,
    and have taken heed of my advérsities.
8 **You have not delivered me into the hand of the énemy;**
    you have set my feet in á broad place.   R

9 Be gracious to me, O Lord, for I am ín distress;
    my eye is wasted from grief,
    my soul and bódy also.
10 **For my life is spént in sorrow,**
    and my yéars with sighing;
 my strength fails because of my mísery,
    and my bones wáste away.
11 I am the scorn of all my adversaries,
    a horror tó my neighbors,
  an object of dread to my acquaintances;
    those who see me in the street flée from me.
12 **I have passed out of mind like one whó is dead;**
    I have become like a bróken vessel.
13 For I hear the whispering of many—
    terror áll around!—
  as they scheme together against me,
    as they plot to táke my life.
14 **But I trust in yóu, O Lord,**
    I say, "You áre my God."
15 My times are ín your hand;
    deliver me from the hand of my enemies and pérsecutors.
16 **Let your face shine ón your servant;**
    save me through your stéadfast love!   R

¹⁷ Do not let me be put to shame, O Lord,
for I cáll on you;
let the wicked be put to shame,
let them go dumbfounded tó Sheol.
¹⁸ **Let the lying líps be mute**
which speak insolently against the righteous
in pride ánd contempt.
¹⁹ O how abundant is your goodness,
which you have laid up for thóse who fear you,
and accomplished for those who take refuge in you,
in the sight of éveryone!
²⁰ **In the protection of your presence you hide them**
from húman plots;
you hold them safe under your shelter
from conténtious tongues.   R

²¹ Blessed bé the Lord
who has wondrously shown steadfast love to me
in a city únder seige.
²² **I had said in mý alarm,**
"I was driven far from your sight."
But you heard my supplications
when I cried to yóu for help.
²³ Love the Lord, all you gódly ones.
The Lord preserves the faithful,
but abundantly repays those who act árrogantly.
²⁴ **Be strong, and let your héart take courage,**
all you who wait fór the Lord!   R

Psalm 32

R

¹ Blessed are those whose transgression ís forgiven,
whose sín is covered.
² **Blessed are those whom the Lord does nót hold guilty,**
and in whose spirit there is nó deceit.
³ When I did not declare my sin, my body wásted away
through my groaning áll day long.
⁴ **For day and night your hand was héavy upon me;**
my strength was dried up as by the héat of summer.
⁵ I acknowledged my sín to you,
and I did not hide my iníquity;
I said, "I will confess my transgressions tó the Lord";
then you forgave the guilt óf my sin.   R

6   Therefore let those who are godly
        offer práyer to you;
  **at a time of distress, the rush of great waters
        shall nót reach them.**
7   You are a hiding place for me,
        you preserve mé from trouble;
        you encompass me with delíverance.
8   **I will instruct you and teach you
        the way yóu should go;
    I will counsel you with my éye upon you.**
9   Do not be like an unruly horse or a mule, without únderstanding,
        whose temper must be curbed with bít and bridle.
10   **Many are the pangs óf the wicked;
        but steadfast love surrounds those who trust ín the Lord.**
11   Be glad in the Lord, and rejóice, O righteous;
        shout for joy, all you upríght in heart!   R

Psalm 33

R

1   Rejoice in the Lord, Ó you righteous!
        Delight in praise, Ó you upright!
2   **Praise the Lord wíth the lyre,
        make melody to the Lord with the harp óf ten strings!**
3   Sing to the Lord á new song,
        play skillfully on the strings, wíth loud shouts.
4   **Upright is the word óf the Lord,
        whose work is done in fáithfulness.   R**

5   The Lord loves justice and ríghteousness;
        the earth is full of the steadfast love óf the Lord.
6   **By the word of the Lord the héavens were made,
        and all their host by the breath óf God's mouth.**
7   The Lord gathered the waters of the sea as ín a bottle
        and put the deeps ín storehouses.
8   **Let all the earth féar the Lord,
        let all the inhabitants of the world stánd in awe!**
9   For the Lord spoke, and it cáme to be,
        the Lord commanded, and ít stood forth.
10   **The Lord brings the counsel of the nátions to nothing
        and frustrates the plans óf the peoples.**
11   The counsel of the Lord stánds forever,
        the thoughts of God's heart to all génerations.
12   **Blessed is the nation whose God ís the Lord,
        the people whom the Lord has chosen as a héritage!   R**

13 The Lord looks down from heaven,
    and sées all peoples;
14 **the Lord sits enthroned and looks forth**
    on all the inhabitants óf the earth,
15 **fashioning the hearts óf them all,**
    and observing áll their deeds.
16 A ruler is not saved by á great army;
    a warrior is not delivered bý great strength.
17 **The war horse is a vain hope for víctory,**
    and despite its great might it cánnot save.
18 Behold, the eye of the Lord is on those whó are faithful,
    and hope for God's stéadfast love
19 to deliver their lífe from death,
    and to keep them alíve in famine.
20 **We wait fór the Lord,**
    who is our hélp and shield.
21 Our heart is glad ín the Lord,
    because we trust in God's hóly name.
22 **Let your steadfast love, O Lord, bé upon us,**
    even as we hópe in you.   **R**

Psalm 34

R

1 I will bless the Lord át all times;
    God's praise shall continually be ín my mouth.
2 **My life makes its boast ín the Lord;**
    let the afflicted hear ánd be glad.
3 O magnify the Lórd with me,
    and let us exalt God's náme together!
4 **I sought the Lord, who ánswered me,**
    and delivered me from áll my fears.
5 Look to God and be rádiant,
    so your faces shall never bé ashamed.
6 **The poor cried out, and thé Lord heard,**
    and saved them out of áll their troubles.
7 The angel of the Lórd encamps
    around those who fear God, and delívers them.
8 **O taste and see that the Lórd is good!**
    Happy are those who take réfuge in God!   **R**

9 O fear the Lord, you hóly ones,
    for those who fear God háve no want!
10 **The young lions suffer wánt and hunger,**
    but those who seek the Lord lack nó good thing.

¹¹ Come, O children, lísten to me,
    I will teach you the fear óf the Lord.
¹² **Which of you desíres life**
    and covets many days to enjóy good?
¹³ Keep your tóngue from evil,
    and your lips from spéaking deceit.
¹⁴ **Depart from evil, ánd do good;**
    seek peace, ánd pursue it.   **R**

¹⁵ The eyes of the Lord are ón the righteous,
    and the ears of the Lord héar their cry.
¹⁶ **The face of the Lord is against évildoers,**
    to cut off the remembrance of them fróm the earth.
¹⁷ When the righteous cry for help, thé Lord hears,
    and delivers them from áll their troubles.
¹⁸ **The Lord is near to the brókenhearted,**
    and saves the crúshed in spirit.
¹⁹ Many are the afflictions óf the righteous;
    but the Lord delivers them fróm them all.
²⁰ **The Lord keeps áll their bones;**
    not one of thém is broken.
²¹ Evil shall sláy the wicked,
    and those who hate the righteous will bé condemned.
²² **The Lord redeems the life óf God's servants;**
    none who take refuge in God will bé condemned.   **R**

Psalm 35

R

¹ Oppose those who oppose mé, O Lord;
    fight against those who fight agáinst me!
² **Take hold of shíeld and buckler,**
    and rise úp to help me!
³ Draw the spear and javelin
    against mý pursuers!
Say to me,
    "I am your delíverance!"   **R**

⁴ Let them be put to shame and dishonor
    who séek my life!
Let them be turned back and confounded
    who devise evil agáinst me!
⁵ **Let them be like chaff before the wind,**
    with the angel of the Lord dríving them!
⁶ **Let their way be dark and slippery,**
    with the angel of the Lord pursúing them!

7 For without cause they hid their nét for me;
    without cause they dug a pit fór my life.
8 **Let ruin come upon them únawares!**
    And let the net that they hid catch them;
    let them fall to rúin in it!
9 Then I shall rejoice ín the Lord,
    exulting in delíverance.
10 **All my bónes shall say,**
    "O Lord, who ís like you?
    You deliver the weak
    from those too stróng for them,
    the weak and needy from those who plúnder them."   **R**

11 Malicious wítnesses rise up;
    they ask me about things I dó not know.
12 **They repay me evil for good;**
    Í am barren.
13 But as for me, when they were sick
    I wore sackcloth,
    I afflicted mysélf with fasting.
    I prayed with head bowed ón my bosom,
14   **as though I grieved for a friend ór a brother;**
    I went about as one who laments fór a mother,
    bowed down ánd in mourning.
15 But at my stumbling they gáthered in glee,
    they gathered together ágainst me;
    ruffians whom I did not know
    tore at me wíthout ceasing;
16 **they impiously mocked more and more,**
    gnashing at me wíth their teeth.   **R**

17 How long, O Lord, will yóu look on?
    Rescue me from their ravages,
    my life fróm the lions!
18 **Then I will thank you in the great cóngregation;**
    in the mighty throng I wíll praise you.
19 Do not let those rejoice over me
    who are my treacherous énemies,
    and do not let those wink the eye
    who hate me wíthout cause.
20 **For they do nót speak peace,**
    but they conceive words of deceit
    against those who are at peace ín the land.
21 They open wide their mouths agáinst me;
    they say, "Aha, Aha!
    Our éyes have seen it!"

22 **You have seen, O Lord; bé not silent!**
      O Lord, be not fár from me!
23 Awake, arise tó my cause;
      to my defense, my God ánd my Lord!
24 **Vindicate me, O Lórd, my God,**
      according to your righteousness;
      and let them not rejoice óver me!
25 Do not let them say to themselves,
      "Aha, we have our héart's desire!"
    Do not let them say, "We have swallowed thát one up."
26 **Let them be put to shame and confusion altogether**
      who rejoice at my calámity.
    Let them be clothed with shame and dishonor
      who magnify themselves ágainst me!   **R**

27 Let those who desire my víndication
      shout for joy and be glad,
      and say évermore,
    "Great is the Lord,
      who delights in the welfare óf this servant."
28 **Then my tongue shall tell of your righteousness**
      and of your praise áll day long.   **R**

Psalm 36

R

1   Transgression speaks to the wicked
      deep ín their hearts;
    there is no fear of God
      befóre their eyes.
2   **For they flatter themselves in théir own eyes**
      that their iniquity cannot be found óut and hated.
3   The words of their mouths are mischief ánd deceit;
      they have ceased to act wisely ánd do good.
4   **They plot mischief while ón their beds;**
      they are set on a way that is not good;
      they do not rejéct evil.   **R**

5   Your steadfast love, O Lord, extends tó the heavens,
      your faithfulness tó the clouds.
6   **Your righteousness is like the míghty mountains,**
      your judgments are like the great deep;
      O Lord, you save humans and ánimals!
7   O God, how precious is your stéadfast love!
      All people may take refuge in the shadow óf your wings.

8 They feast on the abundance óf your house,
   and you give them drink from the river of yóur delights.
9 For with you is the fóuntain of life;
   in your light do wé see light.
10 O continue your steadfast love to thóse who know you,
   and your salvation to the úpright of heart!
11 Do not let the foot of the arrogant cóme upon me.
   nor the hand of the wicked drive mé away.
12 There the evildóers lie prostrate,
   they are thrust down, unáble to rise.   R

Psalm 37

R

1 Do not be angry because óf the wicked,
   do not be envious óf wrongdoers!
2 For they will soon fade líke the grass,
   and wither like thé green herb.
3 Trust in the Lord, ánd do good;
   so you will dwell in the land, and enjoy secúrity.
4 Take delight ín the Lord,
   who will give you the desires óf your heart.   R

5 Commit your way tó the Lord;
   trust in God, whó will act,
6 bringing forth your vindication ás the light,
   and your right as thé noonday.
7 Be still and wait patiently befóre the Lord;
   do not be angry because of those who prosper in their way,
   because of those who carry out évil devices!   R

8 Refrain from anger, and forsáke wrath!
   Do not be angry; it leads ónly to evil.
9 For the wicked shall bé cut off;
   but those who wait for the Lord shall posséss the land.
10 Yet a little while, and the wicked will bé no more;
   though you look at their place, they will nót be there.
11 But the meek shall posséss the land,
   and delight in abundant prospérity.   R

12 The wicked plot agáinst the righteous,
   and gnash their téeth at them;
13 But the Lord laughs át the wicked,
   and sees that their dáy is coming.

14 The wicked draw the sword and bénd their bows,
    to bring down the poor and needy,
    to slay those who walk úprightly;
15 their sword shall enter théir own heart,
    and their bows sháll be broken.　　**R**

16 Better is the little óf the righteous
    than the wealth of mány wicked.
17 For the strength of the wicked sháll be shattered;
    but the Lord uphólds the righteous.
18 **The Lord knows the days óf the blameless,**
    and their heritage abídes forever;
19 **they are not put to shame in évil times,**
    in the days of famine they are sátisfied.
20 But the wícked perish;
    the enemies of the Lord are like burning pastures,
    they vanish—they vánish like smoke.
21 **The wicked borrow, and do nót pay back,**
    but the righteous are génerous and give;
22 **for those blessed by the Lord shall posséss the land,**
    but those cursed by the Lord shall bé cut off.
23 Our steps are made firm bý the Lord,
    who delights ín our way;
24 **though we stumble, we shall not fáll headlong,**
    for the Lord holds us bý the hand.　　**R**

25 I have been young, and nów am old;
    yet I have not seen the righteous forsaken
    or their children bégging bread.
26 **They are ever liberally gíving and lending,**
    and their children becóme a blessing.
27 Depart from evil, ánd do good;
    so you shall abíde forever.
28 For the Lórd loves justice;
    and will not forsáke the faithful.
The righteous shall be kept sáfe forever,
    but the children of the wicked shall bé cut off.
29 **The righteous shall posséss the land,**
    and live in ít forever.
30 The mouths of the righteous útter wisdom,
    and their tóngues speak justice.
31 The law of their God is ín their hearts;
    their steps dó not slip.
32 **The wicked watch for the righteous,**
    and séek to kill them.

33 The Lord will not abandon them to their power,
      or let them be condemned when they are bróught to trial.
34 **Wait for the Lord, and go God's way,**
      who will exalt you to posséss the land;
      you will look on the destruction óf the wicked.   **R**

35 I have seen the wícked oppressing,
      and towering like a cédar of Lebanon.
36 **Again I passed by, and they wére no more;**
      though I sought them, they could nót be found.
37 Mark the blameless, and behold thé upright,
      for there is posterity for the péaceable.
38 **But transgressors shall be altogéther destroyed;**
      the posterity of the wicked shall bé cut off.
39 The salvation of the righteous is fróm the Lord,
      who is their refuge in tíme of trouble.
40 **The Lord helps them and delívers them,**
      delivers them from the wicked and saves them,
      because they take refuge ín the Lord.   **R**

Psalm 38

R

1 O Lord, do not rebuke me ín your anger,
      nor punish me ín your wrath!
2 **For your arrows have sunk ínto me,**
      and your hand has come dówn on me.
3 There is no soundness in my flesh
      because of your índignation;
    there is no health in my bones
      because óf my sin.
4 **For my iniquities have inváded my head;**
      they weigh like a burden too héavy for me.
5 My wounds grow fóul and fester
      because of my fóolishness,
6 **I am utterly bowed dówn and prostrate;**
      all day I gó about mourning.
7 For my loins are fílled with burning,
      and there is no soundness ín my flesh.
8 **I am utterly spént and crushed;**
      I groan because of the tumult óf my heart.   **R**

9 Lord, all my longing is knówn to you,
      my sighing is not hídden from you.
10 **My heart throbs, my stréngth fails me;**
      even the light of my eyes hás gone out.

11 My friends and companions stand aloof fróm my sickness,
and my neighbors stánd far off.

12 **Those who seek my life láy their snares,**
those who seek to hurt me speak of ruin,
and plot treachery áll day long.

13 But I am like the deaf, I dó not hear,
like the mute who dóes not speak.

14 **Truly, I am like one who dóes not hear,**
and in whose mouth is nó retort.   R

15 But I wait for yóu, O Lord;
you will answer, O Lórd, my God!

16 **For I pray, "Let them not rejoice óver me,**
who boast against me when mý foot slips!"

17 For I am réady to fall.
and my pain is éver with me.

18 **I confess my iníquity,**
I am sorry fór my sin.

19 Those who are my foes without cáuse are mighty,
and many are those who hate me wróngfully.

20 **Those who render me évil for good**
oppose me because I follow áfter good.

21 Do not forsake mé, O Lord!
O my God, be not fár from me!

22 **Make haste tó help me,**
O Lord, mý salvation!   R

Psalm 39

R

1 I said, "I will guard my ways,
that I may not sin wíth my tongue;
I will keep a muzzle on my mouth,
so long as the wicked are ín my presence."

2 I was bound with silence,
I was still for the sake óf the right;
my distress grew worse,
my heart burned withín me.

3 In my groaning á fire flamed;
then I spoke wíth my tongue:

4 **"Lord, let me know my end,**
and what is the measure óf my days;
let me know how fleeting mý life is!

5 **You have made my days a few handbreadths,**
and my lifetime is as nothing ín your sight.
Surely every human being is bút a breath!

64

⁶ Surely everyone goes about ás a shadow!
   They are busy for nothing;
   they heap up, but do not know who wíll inherit!   **R**

⁷ "And now, Lord, for what dó I wait?
   My hope ís in you.
⁸ **Deliver me from all my tránsgressions.**
   Do not make me the scorn óf the fool!
⁹ I am silent, I do not ópen my mouth;
   for it is you whó have done it.
¹⁰ **Remove your stróke from me;**
   I am spent by the blows óf your hand.
¹¹ When you chasten people
   with rebúkes for sin,
you consume like a moth what is dear to them;
   surely every human being is bút a breath!
¹² **Hear my prayer, O Lord,**
   and listen tó my cry;
   do not hold your peace át my tears!
For I am your pássing guest,
   like all my áncestors.
¹³ **Look away from me, that I máy know gladness,**
   before I depart and I ám no more!"   **R**

Psalm 40

R

¹ I waited patiently fór the Lord,
   who listened to me and héard my cry.
² **The Lord drew me up from the desolate pit,**
   out of the míry bog,
and set my feet upon a rock,
   making my stéps secure.
³ The Lord put a new song ín my mouth,
   a song of praise tó our God.
Many will see and bé in awe
   and put their trust ín the Lord.   **R**

⁴ Blessed are those who make
   the Lórd their trust,
who do not turn to the proud,
   to those who go astray áfter false gods!
⁵ **O Lord my God, you have multiplied**
   your wondrous deeds and your thóughts toward us;
   none can compáre with you!

         Were I to proclaim and téll of them,
            they would be more than cán be counted.

6 **Sacrifice and offering you do not desire;**
            but you have given me an ópen ear.
         Burnt offering and sin offering
            you have nót required.

7 **Then I said, "Lo, I come;**
            in the roll of the book it is wrítten of me;

8 **I delight to do your will, O my God;**
            your teaching is withín my heart."   **R**

9   I have told the glad news of deliverance
            in the great cóngregation;
         see, I have not restrained my lips,
            as you knów, O Lord.

10 I have not hidden your saving help ín my heart,
            I have spoken of your faithfulness
            and yóur salvation;
         I have not concealed your steadfast love and fáithfulness
            from the great cóngregation.

11 O Lord, do not withhold
            your mércy from me,
         let your steadfast love and faithfulness
            éver preserve me!   **R**

12 For evils have encompassed me
            wíthout number;
         my iniquities have overtaken me,
            until I cánnot see;
            they are more than the hairs óf my head;
            my héart fails me.

13 **Be pleased, O Lord, to delíver me!**
            O Lord, make háste to help me!

14 **Let those be completely shamed ánd confused**
            who seek to snatch awáy my life;
         let those be turned back and brought to dishonor
            who desíre to hurt me!

15 Let those be appalled because of their shame
            who say to me, "Ahá! Aha!"

16 **But may all who seek you**
            rejoice and be glád in you;
         may those who love your salvation
            say continually, "Great ís the Lord!"

17 **As for me, I am póor and needy;**
            but the Lord thínks of me.
         You are my help and my delíverer;
            do not tarry, Ó my God!   **R**

Psalm 41

R

1 Blessed are those who consíder the poor!
The Lord delivers them in the dáy of trouble;
2 **the Lord protects them and keeps thém alive;**
they are called blessed in the land;
you do not give them up to the will óf their enemies.
3 **The Lord sustains them on théir sickbed;**
in their illness you heal all their infírmities.   **R**

4 As for me, I said, "O Lord, be grácious to me;
heal me, for I have sinned ágainst you!"
5 **My enemies wónder in malice**
when I will die, and mý name perish.
6 Those who come to see me utter empty words,
while their hearts gáther mischief;
when they go out, they tell ít abroad.
7 **All who hate me whisper togéther about me;**
they imagine the wórst for me.
8 They think that a deadly thing has fástened on me,
that I will not rise again from whére I lie.
9 **Even my bosom friend in whóm I trusted,**
who ate of my bread, has lifted a heel agáinst me.   **R**

10 But you, O Lord, be grácious to me,
and raise me up, that I may repáy them!
11 **By this I know that you are pléased with me,**
because my enemy has not triumphed óver me.
12 But you have upheld me because of my intégrity,
and set me in your présence forever.
13 **Blessed be the Lord, the God of Ísrael,**
from everlasting to everlasting!
Amen ánd Amen.   **R**

Psalm 42

R

1 As a deer longs for flówing streams,
so I long for yóu, O God.
2 **My whole being thirsts for God,**
for the líving God.
When shall I come and behold
the fáce of God?

67

3 My tears have been my food
    dáy and night,
while people say to me continually,
    "Where ís your God?"
4 These things I remember
    as I pour óut my life:
how I went with the throng,
    and led them in procession to the hóuse of God,
with glad shouts and songs óf thanksgiving,
    a multitude celebrating féstival.
5 **O why am I so burdened,**
    and why am Í so troubled?
Hope in God whom again I shall praise,
6   **my help ánd my God.   R**

My life is cast down upon me,
    therefore I remémber you
    from the land of Jordan and of Hermon, from Móunt Mizar.
7 **Deep calls to deep**
    at the thunder of your cátaracts;
all your waves and your billows
    have gone óver me.
8 By day the Lord commands stéadfast love;
    and at night God's song is with me,
    a prayer to the God óf my life.
9 **I say to God, my rock:**
    "Why have you forgótten me?
Why do I mourn
    because of the enemy's oppréssion?"
10 As with a deadly wound in my body,
    my adversáries taunt me,
while they say to me continually,
    "Where ís your God?"
11 O why am I so burdened,
    and why am Í so troubled?
Hope in God whom again I shall praise,
    my help ánd my God.   R

Psalm 43

R

1 Vindicate me, O God, and defend my cause
    against an ungódly people;
    from the deceitful and unjust delíver me!

2 **For you are the God in whom I take refuge;**
    why have you cást me off?
  Why do I mourn because of the oppression
    of the énemy?

3 O send out your light and your truth;
    let thém lead me,
  let them bring me to your holy hill
    and tó your dwelling!

4 **Then I will go to the altar of God,**
    to God my excéeding joy;
  and I will praise you with the lyre,
    O Gód, my God.

5 **O why am I so burdened,**
    and why am Í so troubled?
  Hope in God whom again I shall praise
    my help ánd my God.   **R**

Psalm 44

R

1 We have heard with our ears, O God,
    our ancestors háve told us,
  what deeds you performed in their days,
    in the dáys of old:

2 **you with your own hand drove out the nations,**
    but our ancéstors you planted;
  you afflicted the peoples,
    but our ancestors yóu set free;

3 for they did not win the land by théir own sword,
    nor did their own arm give them víctory;
  but your right hand, and your arm,
    and the light of your cóuntenance;
    for you delíghted in them.   **R**

4 You are my Ruler ánd my God,
    who ordains víctories for Jacob.

5 **Through you, we push dówn our foes;**
    through your name, we tread down óur assailants.

6 For not in my bow dó I trust,
    nor can my swórd save me.

7 **But you have saved us fróm our foes,**
    and have put to confusion thóse who hate us.

8 **In God we have boasted contínually,**
    and we will give thanks to your náme forever.   **R**

9 Yet you have rejected us and abásed us,
and have not gone out wíth our armies.
10 **You made us turn back fróm the foe;**
and our enemies have gótten spoil.
11 You have made us like shéep for slaughter,
and have scattered us amóng the nations.
12 **You have sold your people fór a trifle,**
demanding no high príce for them.
13 You have made us the taunt óf our neighbors,
the derision and scorn of thóse about us.
14 **You have made us a byword amóng the nations,**
a laughingstock amóng the peoples.   R

15 All day long my disgrace ís before me,
and shame has cóvered my face
16 **at the words of the taunters ánd revilers,**
at the sight of the enemy and thé avenger.
17 All this has come upon us,
yet we have not forgótten you,
or been false to your cóvenant.
18 **Our heart has nót turned back,**
nor have our steps departed fróm your way,
19 **yet you have attacked us in the pláce of monsters,**
and covered us with déep darkness.   R

20 If we had forgotten the name of our God,
or spread forth our hands to á strange god,
21 would not God discover this?
For God knows the secrets óf the heart.
22 **Because of you we are slain áll day long,**
and accounted as sheep fór the slaughter.
23 Rouse yourself! Why do you sléep, O Lord?
Awake! Do not cast us óff forever!
24 **Why do you híde your face?**
Why do you forget our afflication and oppréssion?
25 For we sink down tó the dust;
our bodies cling tó the ground.
26 **Rise up, come tó our help!**
Deliver us for the sake of your stéadfast love!   R

Psalm 45

R

1 My heart overflows with a góodly theme;
  I address my verses to the king;
  my tongue is like the pen of a réady scribe.

2 **You are the most hándsome of men;**
  grace is poured upon your lips;
  therefore God has blessed yóu forever.

3 Gird your sword upon your thigh, O míghty one,
  in your glory and májesty!

4 **In your majesty ride forth victóriously**
  for the cause of truth and to defend the right;
  let your right hand teach yóu dread deeds!

5 Your arrows are sharp
  in the heart of the king's énemies;
  the peoples fall únder you.

6 **Your throne, O God, endures foréver and ever.**
  Your royal scepter is a scepter of equity;

7 **you love righteousness and hate wíckedness.**
  Therefore God, your God, has anointed you
  with the oil of gladness abóve your peers;

8 your robes are all fragrant with myrrh and aloes and cássia.
  From ivory palaces stringed instruments máke you glad;

9 **daughters of kings are among your ladies of honor;**
  at your right hand stands the queen in góld of Ophir.   **R**

10 Hear, O daughter, consider and listen;
   forget your people and your fáther's house;

11 and the king will desíre your beauty.
   Since he is your lord, bów to him;

12 the people of Tyre will seek your favor with gifts,
   the richest of the people

13 with all kínds of wealth.
   The princess in her chamber is decked with gold-wóven robes;

14 **in many-colored robes she is led to the king;**
   behind her the virgins, her compánions, follow.

15 **With joy and gladness they are léd along**
   as they enter the palace óf the king.

16 In the place of ancestors you sháll have sons;
   you will make them princes in áll the earth.

17 **I will cause your name to be celebrated in all génerations;**
   therefore the peoples will praise you foréver and ever.   **R**

71

Psalm 46

R

¹ God is our refúge and strength,
a very present hélp in trouble.

² **Therefore we will not fear through the éarth should change,**
though the mountains shake in the heart óf the sea;

³ though its waters róar and foam,
though the mountains tremble wíth its tumult.

⁴ **There is a river whose streams make glad the cíty of God,**
the holy habitation of thé Most High.

⁵ God is in the midst of the city which shall nót be moved;
God will help it when mórning dawns.

⁶ **The nations rage, the kíngdoms totter;**
God's voice resounds, thé earth melts.

⁷ The Lord of hósts is with us;
the God of Jacob ís our refuge.   R

⁸ Come, behold the works óf the Lord,
who has brought wonders tó the earth;

⁹ **who makes wars cease to the end óf the earth,**
breaks the bow, shatters the spear,
and burns the shíelds with fire!

¹⁰ "Be still, and know that Í am God.
I am exalted among the nations,
I am exalted ín the earth!"

¹¹ **The Lord of hósts is with us;**
the God of Jacob ís our refuge.   R

Psalm 47

R

¹ Clap your hands, all peoples!
Shout to God with loud sóngs of joy!

² For the Lord, the Most High, is to be feared,
a great Ruler over áll the earth,

³ who subdued peoples under us,
and nations únder our feet,

⁴ **who chose our heritage for us,**
the pride of Jacob whóm God loves.   R

⁵ God has gone up wíth a shout,
the Lord with the sound óf a trumpet.

⁶ Sing praises to Gód, sing praises!
Sing praises to our Rúler, sing praises!

⁷ For God is the Ruler of áll the earth;
sing praises wíth a psalm!

⁸ God reigns óver the nations;
God sits on a hóly throne.

9 The princes of the people gather
    as the people of the God of Ábraham.
For the shields of the earth belong to God,
    who is híghly exalted!   **R**

Psalm 48

R

1 Great is the Lord and greatly tó be praised
    in the city óf our God;
2 **whose holy mountain, beautiful in élevation,**
    is the joy of áll the earth,
Mount Zion, in the far north,
    the city of thé great Ruler.
3 **Within its citadels God**
    has proven a súre defense.   **R**

4 See how the kings assembled
    and márched together.
5 **As soon as they saw it, they were astounded,**
    they were in panic, they tóok to flight;
6 trembling took hold of them there,
    anguish as of a wóman in labor,
7 **as when an east wind shatters**
    the shíps of Tarshish.
8 As we have heard, so have we seen
    in the city of the Lórd of hosts,
in the city of our God,
    which God establishes foréver.
9 **We ponder your steadfast lóve, O God,**
    in the midst óf your temple.   **R**

10 As your name, O God,
    so your praise reaches to the ends óf the earth.
Your right hand is filled with victory;
11   **let Mount Zíon be glad!**
Let the daughters of Judah rejoice
    because óf your judgments!
12 **Walk around Zion, go round about it,**
    númber its towers,
13 consider well its ramparts,
    go through its cítadels,
    that you may tell the next géneration,
14 **"This is God,**
    our God foréver and ever.
    God will be our guíde forever."   **R**

Psalm 49

R

¹ Hear this, all peoples!
    Listen, all inhabitants óf the world,
² both low and high,
    rich and póor together!
³ **My mouth sháll speak wisdom;**
    the meditation of my heart shall be únderstanding.
⁴ **I will pay attention tó a proverb;**
    I will solve my riddle to the music óf the harp.   R

⁵ Why should I fear in tímes of trouble,
    when the iniquity of my persecutors surróunds me,
⁶ those who trust ín their wealth
    and boast of the abundance óf their riches?
⁷ **Truly, no ransom avails fór one's life,**
    there is no price one can give to Gód for it,
⁸ for the ransom of life is costly,
    and can néver suffice,
⁹ that one should live on forever
    and never sée the grave.
¹⁰ **Consider the wíse, they die;**
    the stupid and the foolish perish together
    and leave their wéalth to others.
¹¹ Their graves are their hómes forever,
    their dwelling places to all generations,
    though they named lánds their own.
¹² **Mortals cannot abide ín their pomp,**
    they are like ánimals that perish.   R

¹³ Such is the fate of thé foolhardy,
    the end of those who are pleased wíth their lot.
¹⁴ **Like sheep they are appóinted for Sheol;**
    death shall bé their shepherd;
    straight to the grave they descend,
        and their form shall wáste away;
        Sheol shall bé their home.
¹⁵ **But God will ransom my soul from the pówer of Sheol,**
    and wíll receive me.   R

¹⁶ Do not be afraid when some becóme rich,
    when the wealth of their hóuses increases.
¹⁷ **For when they die they will carry nóthing away;**
    their wealth will not gó with them.
¹⁸ Though, in their lifetime, they count thémselves happy
        —for you are praised when you do well fór yourself—
¹⁹ they will go to the company of their áncestors,
    who will never again sée the light.
²⁰ **Mortals cannot abide ín their pomp,**
    they are like ánimals that perish.   R

Psalm 50

R

¹ The Mighty One, Gód the Lord,
    speaks and summons the earth
    from the rising of the sun tó its setting.
² **Out of Zion, the perfection of beauty,**
    Gód shines forth.
³ Our God comes, and does not keep silence,
    before whom is a devouring fire,
    round about whom is a míghty storm.
⁴ **God calls to the héavens above**
    and to the earth, in order to júdge the people:
⁵ "Gather to me my fáithful ones,
    who made a covenant with me by sácrifice!"
⁶ **The heavens declare God's ríghteousness,**
    for God alóne is judge!   R

⁷ "Listen, my people, and I will speak:
    I will testify against you, O Ísrael.
    I am Gód, your God.
⁸ **I do not reprove you for your sácrifices;**
    your burnt offerings are continually befóre me.
⁹ But I will not accept a bull fróm your house,
    nor goats fróm your pens.
¹⁰ **For every beast of the fórest is mine,**
    the cattle on a thóusand hills.
¹¹ I know all the birds óf the air,
    and all that moves in the fíeld is mine.
¹² **If I were hungry, I wóuld not tell you,**
    for the world and all that is in ít is mine.
¹³ Do I eat the flésh of bulls,
    or drink the blóod of goats?
¹⁴ **Offer to God a sacrifice óf thanksgiving,**
    and pay your vows to thé Most High;
¹⁵ **and call upon me in the dáy of trouble;**
    I will deliver you, and you shall glórify me."   R

¹⁶ But to the wicked God says:
    "What right have you to recíte my statutes,
    or take my covenant ón your lips?
¹⁷ **For you hate discipline,**
    and you cast my wórds behind you.
¹⁸ You make friends with thieves when you see them,
    and you keep company with adúlterers.

19 **You give your mouth free réign for evil,**
  and your tongue fråmes deceit.
20 You sit and speak agáinst your brother;
  you slander your móther's son.
21 **These things you have done and I have been silent;**
  you thought that I was one líke yourself.
  But now I rebuke you, and lay the chárge before you.
22 You who forget Gód, mark this,
  or I will tear you apart, and no one wíll save you!
23 **Those who bring thanksgiving as their sacrifice hónor me;**
  to those who go the right way,
  I will show the salvátion of God!" **R**

Psalm 51

R

1 Have mercy on me, O God,
  according to your stéadfast love;
  according to your abundant mercy
  blot out mý transgressions.
2 Wash me thoroughly from my iníquity,
  and cleanse me fróm my sin!
3 **For I know my transgressions,**
  and my sin is éver before me.
4 Against you, you only, Í have sinned,
  and done that which is evil ín your sight,
  so that you are justified ín your sentence
  and blameless ín your judgment.
5 **Indeed, I was born into iníquity,**
  and I have been sinful since my mother concéived me. **R**

6 Surely, you desire truth in the ínward being;
  therefore teach me wisdom in my sécret heart.
7 **Purge me with hyssop, and I sháll be clean;**
  wash me, and I shall be whíter than snow;
8 Let me hear with jóy and gladness;
  let the bones which you have bróken rejoice.
9 **Hide your face fróm my sins,**
  and blot out all my iníquities. **R**

10 Create in me a clean héart, O God,
  and put a new and right spírit within me.
11 **Cast me not away fróm your presence,**
  and take not your holy spírit from me.
12 Restore to me the joy of yóur salvation,
  and sustain in me a wílling spirit.

13 **Then I will teach transgréssors your ways,**
   and sinners will retúrn to you.
14 Deliver me from bloodshed, O God, God of mý salvation,
   and my tongue will sing aloud of your delíverance.
15 **O Lord, ópen my lips,**
   and my mouth shall show fórth your praise.
16 For you have no delight in sácrifice;
   were I to give a burnt offering, you would nót be pleased.
17 **The sacrifice acceptable to God is a bróken spirit;**
   a broken and contrite heart, O God, you will nót despise.
18 Do good to Zion in yóur good pleasure;
   rebuild the walls of Jerúsalem;
19 **then you will delight in right sacrifices,**
   in burnt offerings and whole burnt ófferings;
   then bulls will be offered ón your altar.   R

Psalm 52

R

1 Why do you boast, O mighty one,
   of mischief done agáinst the godly?
   All day long
2 you are plotting destrúction.
   Your tongue is sharp líke a razor,
   you worker of tréachery.
3 You love evil móre than good,
   and lying more than spéaking the truth.
4 **You love all words thát devour,**
   O decéitful tongue.   R

5 But God will break you dówn forever,
   will snatch and tear you from your tent,
   will uproot you from the land óf the living.
6 **The righteous shall sée, and fear,**
   and shall laugh at the evildóer, saying,
7 **"See the one who would not take**
   réfuge in God,
   but trusted in abundant riches,
   and sought réfuge in wealth!"   R

8 But I am like a green olive tree
   in the hóuse of God.
   I trust in the steadfast love of God
   forevér and ever.

9 I will thank you forever,
      because of what yóu have done.
   In the presence of the faithful
      I will proclaim your name, for ít is good.   **R**

Psalm 53

R

1 Fools say in their hearts,
      "There ís no God."
   They are corrupt, they do abominable deeds;
      there is none whó does good.
2 God looks down from heaven ón all people
      to see if there are any who are wise,
      any who seek áfter God.
3 **They have all fallen away;**
      they are all alíke perverse;
   there is none who does good,
      nó, not one.   R

4 Have they no knowledge, the évildoers,
      who eat up my people as they eat bread,
      and do not cáll upon God?
5 **There they shall be ín great terror,**
      in terror such as hás not been!
   For God will scatter the bones of thé ungodly;
      they will be put to shame, for God has rejécted them.
6 O that deliverance for Israel would cóme from Zion!
      When God restores their fortunes,
      Jacob shall rejoice, Israel sháll be glad.   R

Psalm 54

R

1 Save me, O God, bý your name,
      and vindicate me bý your might.
2 **Hear my práyer, O God;**
      listen to the words óf my mouth.
3 For the insolent have rísen against me,
      the ruthless seek my life;
      they do not set God befóre them.
4 **But surely, God ís my helper;**
      the Lord is the upholder óf my life.
5 God will repay my enemies fór their evil.
      In your faithfulness, put an énd to them.

78

6 With a freewill offering I will sacrifíce to you;
   I will give thanks to your name, O Lord, for ít is good.
7 For God has delivered me from évery trouble,
   and my eye has looked in triumph ón my enemies.   **R**

Psalm 55

R

1 Hear my práyer, O God;
   do not hide yourself from my súpplication!
2 Attend to me, and ánswer me;
   I am troubled in mý complaint.
I am distraught
3 **by the noise of the énemy,**
   because of the clamor óf the wicked.
For they bring trouble upón me,
   and in anger théy hate me.
4 My heart is in anguish within me,
   the terrors of death have fállen upon me.
5 Fear and trembling come upon me,
   and horror óverwhelms me.
6 **And I say, "O that I had wings líke a dove!**
   I would fly away and bé at rest;
7 **Truly, I would flee fár away,**
   I would lodge in the wílderness,
8 **I would hasten to fínd a shelter**
   from the raging wínd and tempest."   **R**

9 Confuse, O Lord, confóund their speech;
   for I see violence and strife ín the city.
10 **Day and night they go around it**
   ón its walls;
and iniquity and trouble áre within it,
11   **ruin is ín its midst;**
oppression and fraud
   do not depart from its márket place.
12 It is not enemies who taunt me—
   I cóuld bear that;
it is not adversaries who deal insolently with me—
   I could híde from them.
13 But it is you, my equal,
   my companion, my famíliar friend,
14 **with whom I kept pleasant company;**
   we walked in the house of God wíth the throng.

79

¹⁵ Let death come upon them;
　　　let them go down alíve to Sheol;
　　　for evil is in their homes and ín their hearts.
¹⁶ **But I call upón God;**
　　　and the Lórd will save me.　R

¹⁷ Evening and morning and at noon
　　　I utter my compláint and moan,
　　　and God will héar my voice.
¹⁸ **God will redeem mé unharmed**
　　　from the battle that I wage,
　　　for many are arrayed agáinst me.
¹⁹ God, who is enthroned from of old,
　　　will hear, and will húmble them,
　　　because they do not change,
　　　and do nót fear God.
²⁰ **My companion laid hands on a friend**
　　　and violated a cóvenant with me
²¹ **with speech smoother than butter,**
　　　but with a heart sét on war;
　　　with words that were sófter than oil,
　　　but in fact wére drawn swords.
²² Cast your burden ón the Lord,
　　　who will sustain you,
　　　and will never permit the righteous tó be moved.
²³ **But you, O God, will cást them down**
　　　into the lówest pit;
　　　the bloodthirsty and treacherous
　　　shall not live out hálf their days.
　　　But I will trúst in you.　R

Psalm 56

R

¹ Be gracious to me, O God, for people trámple on me;
　　　all day long foes oppréss me;
² my enemies trample on me áll day long,
　　　for many fight agáinst me.
³ **O Most High, when I am afraid, I put my trúst in you.**
⁴ **In God, whose word I praise,**
　　　in God I trust; I am not afraid.
　　　What can flesh dó to me?　R

⁵ All day long they seek to ínjure my cause;
　　　all their thoughts are against mé for evil.

6 **They stir up strífe, they lurk,**
   they wátch my steps.
   As they hoped to have my life,
7   so repay them fór their crime;
      in wrath cast down the péoples, O God!
8 **You have witnessed my trembling,**
   stored my tears ín your bottle.
   Are they not ín your book?
9 Then my enemies will retreat
      in the day whén I call.
      This I know, that God ís for me.
10 **In God, whose wórd I praise,**
    in the Lord whose wórd I praise,
11 **in God I trust; I am nót afraid.**
    What can a mere mortal dó to me?
12 I must perform my vows to yóu , O God;
      I will render thank ófferings to you.
13 **For you have delivered my soul from death,**
    and my féet from falling,
   so that I may walk before God
      in the líght of life.   R

Psalm 57

R

1 Be merciful to me, O God, be merciful to me,
      for in you Í take refuge;
   in the shadow of your wings I will take refuge,
      till the storms of destrúction pass by.
2 I cry to God Most High,
      to Gód who shields me,
3 **who will send from heaven and save me,**
      who will put to shame those who trample upón me.
      God will send forth stéadfast love and fáithfulness!
4 I lie down among lions
      that devour húman prey;
   their teeth are spears and arrows,
      their tóngues sharp swords.
5 **Be exalted, O God, abóve the heavens!**
      Let your glory be over áll the earth!   R

6 They set a net for my steps;
      my lífe was trapped.
   They dug a pit in my way,
      but they have fallen into ít themselves.

7 My heart is steadfast, O God,
  my héart is steadfast!
  I will sing and make mélody!
8 **Awáke, my soul!**
  Awake, O harp and lyre!
  I will awáke the dawn!
9 **I will give thanks to you, O Lord, amóng the peoples;**
  I will sing praises to you amóng the nations.
10 For your steadfast love is vast ás the heavens,
  your faithfulness extends tó the clouds.
11 **Be exalted, O God, abóve the heavens!**
  Let your glory be over áll the earth!   **R**

Psalm 58

R

1 Do you indeed decree what is ríght, you gods?
  Do you judge mórtals fairly?
2 **No, in your hearts you devíse wrongs;**
  your hands deal out víolence on earth.
3 The wicked go astray fróm the womb,
  they err from their birth, spéaking lies.
4 **They have venom like the venom óf a serpent,**
  like the deaf adder that stóps its ear,
5 **so that it does not hear the vóice of charmers**
  or of the cúnning enchanter.   **R**

6 O God, break the teeth ín their mouths;
  tear out the fangs of the young líons, O Lord!
7 **Let them vanish like water that rúns away;**
  let them be trodden down and wíther like grass.
8 Let them be like the snail that dissolves ínto slime,
  like the untimely birth that never sées the sun.
9 **Sooner than your pots can feel the héat of thorns,**
  whether green or ablaze, may God sweep thém away!
10 The righteous will rejoice when they see véngeance done;
  they will bathe their feet in the blood óf the wicked.
11 **People will say, "Surely there is a reward fór the righteous;**
  surely there is a God who júdges on earth."   **R**

Psalm 59

R

1 Deliver me from my enemies, Ó my God,
  protect me from those who rise úp against me.

2 Deliver me from those whó work evil,
   from the bloodthírsty save me.
3 **Even now they lie in wait fór my life;**
   the mighty stir up strife against me.
   For no transgression or sin of míne, O Lord,
4 **for no fault of mine, they run ánd make ready.**
   Rouse yourself, come to my hélp and see!
5 You, Lord God of hosts, are God of Ísrael.
   Awake to punish áll the nations;
   spare none of those who treacherously plót evil.
6 **Each evening théy come back,**
   howling like dogs
   and prowling abóut the city.
7 There they are, bellowing with their mouths,
   with sharp words ón their lips—
   for they think "Who wíll hear us?"
8 **But you laugh at thém, O Lord;**
   you hold all the nations ín derision.
9 O my strength, I will wátch for you;
   for you are my fórtress, O God.
10 **My God will meet me in stéadfast love;**
    my God will let me look in triumph on my énemies.   R

11 Do not kill them, or my people máy forget;
    make them totter by your power, and bring them down,
    O Lórd, our shield!
12 **For the sin of their mouths, the words óf their lips,**
    let them be trapped ín their pride.
    For the cursing and lies that they utter,
13 consume thém in wrath,
    consume them until they áre no more.
    Then it will be known to the ends óf the earth
    that God rules óver Jacob.
14 Each evening théy come back,
    howling like dogs
    and prowling abóut the city.
15 **They roam abóut for food,**
    and growl if they do not gét their fill.
16 But I will sing óf your might;
    I will sing aloud of your steadfast love ín the morning.
    For you have been a fórtress to me
    and a refuge in the day of mý distress.
17 **O my strength, I will sing práises to you,**
    for you are my fortress, O God,
    the God who shows me stéadfast love.   R

Psalm 60

R

1 O God, you have rejected us, broken óur defenses;
   you have been angry; restóre us!
2 **You have caused the land to quake, you have tórn it open;**
   repair the cracks in it, for it is tóttering.
3 You have made your people súffer hard things;
   you have given us wine to drink that máde us reel.
4 **You have set up a banner for those who fear you,**
   to escápe the bow.
5 **Deliver with your right hand, and answer us,**
   that those whom you love máy be rescued. **R**

6 **God has spoken in hóliness:**
   "With exultation I will divide up Shechem,
   and portion out the pláin of Succoth.
7 **Gilead is mine; Manássah is mine;**
   Ephraim is my helmet;
   Judah ís my scepter.
8 **Moab is my washbasin;**
   on Edom I húrl my shoe;
   over Philistia I shóut in triumph."
9 Who will bring me to the fórtified city?
   Who will lead mé to Edom?
10 **Have you not rejected ús, O God?**
   You do not go out, O God, wíth our armies.
11 O grant us help agáinst the foe,
   for human hélp is worthless.
12 **With God we shall do váliantly;**
   it is God who will tread dówn our foes. **R**

Psalm 61

R

1 Hear my cry, O God,
   listen tó my prayer;
2 **from the end of the earth I call to you,**
   when my héart is faint.
3 Lead me to the rock that is hígher than I;
   for you are my refuge,
   a strong tower against the énemy.
4 **Let me dwell in your tént forever,**
   find refuge under the shelter óf your wings.

⁵ For you, O God, have héard my vows,
   you have given me the heritage of those who féar your name.
⁶ **Prolong the life óf the king;**
   may his years endure to all génerations!
⁷ May he be enthroned forever befóre God;
   appoint steadfast love and faithfulness to watch óver him!
⁸ **So I will always sing praises tó your name,**
   as I pay my vows day áfter day.   R

Psalm 62

R

¹ In silence I wait for Gód alone,
   from whom my salvátion comes.
² **God alone is my rock and mý salvation,**
   my fortress; I shall néver be shaken.
³ How long will you assail a person,
   will you batter your victim, áll of you,
   as you would a leaning wall, a tóttering fence?
⁴ **They scheme to drag péople down;**
   they take pléasure in lies.
   They bless wíth their mouths,
   inwardlý they curse.
⁵ **In silence I wait for God alone,**
   for my hope ís from God,
⁶ **who alone is my rock and my salvation,**
   my fortress; I shall nót be shaken.
⁷ On God rests my deliverance ánd my honor;
   my mighty rock, my réfuge is God.
⁸ **Trust in God at all tímes, O people;**
   pour out your heart before God
   who ís our refuge.   R

⁹ Those of low estate are bút a breath,
   those of high estate are á delusion;
   in the balances théy go up;
   they are together lighter thán a breath.
¹⁰ **Put no confidence in extortion,**
   set no vain hopes on róbbery;
   if riches increase, set not your héart on them.
¹¹ Once God has spoken,
   twice I háve heard this:
   power belóngs to God;
¹² **and to you belongs steadfast lóve, O Lord,**
   for you repay all
   according tó their work.   R

Psalm 63

R

1 O God, you are my God, Í seek you,
      I thírst for you;
   my flesh fáints for you,
      as in a dry and weary land where no wáter is.
2 **So I have looked upon you in the sánctuary,**
      beholding your pówer and glory.
3 Because your steadfast love is bétter than life,
      my lips wíll praise you.
4 **So I will bless you as long ás I live;**
      I will lift up my hands and call ón your name.   **R**

5 My soul is feasted as with márrow and fat,
      and my mouth praises you with jóyful lips,
6 when I think of you upón my bed,
      and meditate on you in the watches óf the night;
7 **for you have béen my help,**
      and in the shadow of your wings I síng for joy.
8 **My soul clíngs to you;**
      your right hánd upholds me.   **R**

9 But those who seek to destroy my life
      shall go down into the depths óf the earth;
10 **they shall be given over to the power of the sword,**
      they shall be préy for jackals.
11 But the monarch shall rejóice in God;
      all who swear in God's name shall glory;
      but the mouths of liars wíll be stopped.   **R**

Psalm 64

R

1 Hear the voice of my compláint, O God;
      preserve my life from the dread énemy.
2 **Hide me from the secret plots óf the wicked,**
      from the scheming of évildoers,
3 who whet their tóngues like swords,
      who aim bitter wórds like arrows,
4 **shooting from ambush át the blameless;**
      they shoot suddenly and wíthout fear.
5 They hold fast to their évil purpose;
      they talk of laying snares sécretly,
      thinking,

86

6 "Who cán see us?
    Who can search óut our crimes?
    We have thought out a cunningly concéived plot."
    For the human heart and mínd are deep!

7 But God will shoot an árrow at them;
    they will be wounded súddenly.

8 **God will bring them to ruin because óf their tongue;**
    all who see them will sháke with horror.

9 Then everyóne will fear;
    they will tell what God has brought about,
    and ponder what Gód has done.

10 **Let the righteous rejoice,**
    and take refuge ín the Lord.
    Let all the upright in héart glory!   R

Psalm 65

R

1 Praise is due to you,
    O Gód in Zion;
    to you vows shall bé performed.

2 **Because óf their sins,**
    all flesh shall come to you
    whó hear prayer.

3 When our transgressions prevail óver us,
    you forgíve them.

4 **Blessed are those whom you choose and bring near,**
    to dwell ín your courts!
    We shall be satisfied with the goodness of your house,
    your hóly temple!   R

5 By dread deeds you answer us with delíverance,
    O God of óur salvation,
    who is the hope of all the ends óf the earth,
    and of the fárthest seas.

6 **By your strength you estáblished the mountains;**
    you are gírded with might.

7 You still the roaring óf the seas,
    the roaring of the waves,
    the tumult óf the peoples,

8 so that those who dwell at earth's farthest bounds
    are afraid át your signs;
    you make the morning and the
    evening resóund with joy.   R

⁹ You visit the earth and wáter it,
  you gréatly enrich it;
  the river of God is fúll of water;
  you provide its grain,
  for so you háve prepared it.

¹⁰ You water its furrows abúndantly,
   settling its ridges,
   softening it with showers,
   and bléssing its growth.

¹¹ **You crown the year wíth your bounty;**
   the tracks of your chariot dríp with fatness.

¹² The pastures of the wilderness drip,
   the hills gird themsélves with joy,

¹³ **the meadows clothe themselves with flocks,**
   the valleys deck themselves with grain,
   they shout and sing togéther for joy.   **R**

Psalm 66

R

¹ Make a joyful noise to God, áll the earth;

² sing the glory of God's name;
  give to God glórious praise!

³ **Say to God, "How awesome áre your deeds!**
  Because of your great power, your enemies crínge before you.

⁴ All the earth wórships you;
  they sing praises to you,
  sing praises tó your name."

⁵ **Come and see what Gód has done:**
  God is awesome in deeds amóng mortals.

⁶ God turned the sea ínto dry land;
  they passed through the ríver on foot.

⁷ **There we rejoiced in God**
  who rules by míght forever,
  whose eyes keep watch on the nations—
  let the rebellious not exált themselves.   **R**

⁸ Bless our God, O peoples,
  let the sound of God's práise be heard,

⁹ who has kept us among the living,
  and has not let óur feet slip.

¹⁰ **For you, O God, have tésted us;**
   you have tried us as sílver is tried.

11   You brought us ínto the net;
      you laid burdens ón our backs;
12   **you let people ride óver our heads;**
      we went through fire and through water;
      yet you have brought us out to a spácious place.
13   I will come into your house wíth burnt offerings;
      I will pay yóu my vows,
14   those which mý lips uttered
      and my mouth promised when I wás in trouble.
15   **I will offer to you burnt offerings of fatlings,**
      with the smoke of the sacrifíce of rams;
      I will make an offering of búlls and goats.   **R**

16   Come and hear, all you who wórship God,
      and I will tell what God has dóne for me.
17   **I cried alóud to God,**
      who was highly praised wíth my tongue.
18   If I had cherished iniquity ín my heart,
      the Lord would nót have listened.
19   **But truly Gód has listened,**
      and has given heed to the voice óf my prayer.
20   **Blessed be God,**
      who has not rejécted my prayer
      or removed steadfast lóve from me.   **R**

Psalm 67

R

1   O God, be gracious to ús and bless us
      and make your face to shine upón us,
2   **that your way may be known upón earth,**
      your saving power amóng all nations.
3   Let the peoples praise yóu, O God,
      let all the péoples praise you!
4   **Let the nations be glad and síng for joy,**
      for you judge the peoples with equity
      and guide the nations upón earth.   **R**

5   Let the peoples praise yóu, O God;
      let all the péoples praise you!
6   **The earth has yielded íts increase;**
      God, our God, hás blessed us.
7   May Gód bless us;
      let all the ends of the éarth fear God!   **R**

Psalm 68

R

1 Let God arise, let God's énemies be scattered;
    let those who háte God flee!

2 **As smoke is driven away, so drive thém away;**
    as wax melts before fire,
    let the wicked perish befóre God!

3 But let the ríghteous be joyful;
    let them rejoice before God;
    let them be jubilánt with joy!

4 **Sing to God, sing praises tó God's name;**
    lift a song to the One who rides upon the clouds;
    rejoice before the One whose náme is Lord!   **R**

5 In the holy habitation God is the fáther of orphans
    and protéctor of widows.

6 **God gives the desolate a home in which to dwell,**
    and leads out the prisoners to prospérity;
    but the rebellious dwell in á parched land.

7 O God, when you went forth befóre your people,
    when you marched through the wílderness,

8 **the earth quaked, the heavens póured down water,**
    at the presence of God, the God of Sinai,
    at the presence of God, the God of Ísrael.

9 You showered abundant ráin, O God;
    you restored your heritage ás it languished;

10 **your flock found a dwélling in it;**
    in your goodness, O God, you provided fór the needy.

11 The Lord gives thé command;
    great is the company of those who bore the tidings:
    "the kings of the armies, they flée, they flee!"

12 **The women at home divíde the spoil,**
    though they stay amóng the sheepfolds—

13 the wings of a dove cóvered with silver,
    its pinions wíth green gold.

14 **When the Almighty scáttered kings there,**
    snow féll on Zalmon.   **R**

15 O mighty mountain, mountain óf Bashan;
    O many-peaked mountain, mountain óf Bashan!

16 **Why do you look with envy, O mány-peaked mountain,**
    at the mount that God desired for an abode,
    where the Lord will resíde forever?

17 With mighty chariotry, twice ten thousand,
    thousands upón thousands,

the Lord came from Sinai into the hóly place.
18 **You ascended thé high mount,**
leading captives ín your train,
receiving tribute from the people,
even the rebéllious ones.
The Lórd God lives!
19 Blessed be the Lord,
who daily béars us up;
God is óur salvation.
20 **Our God is a God óf salvation;**
and to God, the Lord, belongs escápe from death.   **R**

21 But God will shatter the heads of énemies,
the hairy crown of those who walk in their guílty ways.
22 **The Lord said,**
"I will bring them báck from Bashan,
I will bring them back from the depths óf the sea,
23 **so that you may bathe your féet in blood,**
so that the tongues of your dogs may have their share fróm
the foe."
24 Your solemn processions are séen, O God;
the processions of my God, my Ruler, into the sánctuary—
25 the singers in front, the hárpists last,
and between them girls playing támbourines:
26 **"Bless God in the great cóngregation,**
The Lord, O you who are of Ísrael's fountain!"
27 There is Benjamin, the least of them, ín the lead,
the princes of Judah in a body,
the princes of Zebulun, the princes of Náphtali.
28 **Summon your míght, O God;**
show your strength, O God, as you have done for ús before.
29 Because of your temple at Jerúsalem
rulers bear gífts to you.
30 **Rebuke the wild animals that live amóng the reeds,**
the herd of bulls with the calves óf the peoples.
Trample under foot those who lust áfter tribute;
scatter the peoples who delíght in war.
31 **Let bronze be bróught from Egypt;**
let Ethiopia hasten to stretch out its hánds to God.
32 Sing to God, O realms óf the earth;
sing praises tó the Lord.
33 **O Rider in the heavens, the áncient heavens,**
God's voice goes forth, a míghty voice.
34 Ascribe power to God,
whose majesty is over Ísrael,
and whose power is ín the skies.

35 **Wondrous is God in the sánctuary,**
   the God of Israel,
   who gives power and strength tó the people.   **R**

Psalm 69

R

1   Save me, O God!
     For the waters have come up tó my neck.
2   **I sink in deep mire,**
     where there is nó foothold;
   I have come intó deep waters,
     and the flood sweeps óver me.
3   I am weary with crying;
     my thróat is parched.
   My eyes grow dim
     with waiting fór my God.
4   **More in number than the hairs óf my head**
     are those who hate me wíthout cause;
   many are those who wóuld destroy me,
     my enemies who accúse me falsely.
   What I did not steal
     must I nów restore?
5   **O God, you know my folly;**
     the wrongs I have done are not hídden from you.
6   O Lord God of hosts,
     do not let those who hope in you be shámed through me;
   O God of Israel,
     do not let those who seek you be dishónored through me.
7   It is for your sake that I have bórne insult,
     that shame has cóvered my face.
8   **I have become a stranger tó my brothers,**
     an alien to my móther's children.   **R**

9   Zeal for your house hás consumed me,
     and the insults of those who insult you have fállen on me.
10 **When I humbled mysélf with fasting,**
     it became an ínsult to me.
11 When I made sáckcloth my clothing,
     I became a jóke to them.
12 **I am the talk of those who sit ín the gate,**
     and the drunkards make songs abóut me.
13 But as for me, my prayer is to yóu, O Lord.
     At an acceptable time, O God,

in the abundance of your steadfast love, ánswer me.

14 **With your faithful help rescue me**
from sinking ín the mire;
let me be delivered from my enemies
and from thé deep waters.

15 **Do not let the flood sweep óver me,**
or the deep swallow me up,
or the pit close its mouth óver me. **R**

16 Answer me, O Lord, for your steadfast lóve is good;
turn to me according to your abúndant mercy.

17 **Do not hide your face fróm your servant,**
for I am in distress—make haste to ánswer me.

18 Draw near to mé, redeem me,
set me free because of my énemies!

19 **You know the insults Í receive,**
my shame and dishonor;
my foes are all knówn to you.

20 Insults have bróken my heart,
so that I am ín despair;
I looked for pity, but thére was none;
and for comforters, but Í found none.

21 They gave me póison for food,
and gave me vinegar to drink fór my thirst.

22 **Let their table be a tráp for them,**
a snare for théir allies.

23 Let their eyes be darkened, so that they cánnot see;
and make their loins tremble contínually.

24 **Pour out your indignation upón them,**
and let your burning anger overtáke them.

25 May their camp be a désolation,
let no one live ín their tents,

26 for they persecute those whom you háve struck down,
and they attack still more those whom yóu have wounded.

27 **Add guilt tó their guilt;**
may they have no acqúittal from you.

28 Let them be blotted out of the book óf the living;
let them not be enrolled amóng the righteous.

29 **But I am lowly ánd in pain;**
let your salvation, O God, protéct me! **R**

30 I will praise the name of God wíth a song;
I will magnify God wíth thanksgiving.

31 **This will please the Lord more thán an ox**
or a bull with hórns and hoofs.

32   Let the oppressed see it ánd be glad;
      you who seek God, let your héarts revive.
33   **For the Lord héars the needy,**
      and does not despise God's own who áre in bonds.
34   Let heaven and earth práise the Lord.
      the seas and everything that móves in them.
35   **For God wíll save Zion**
      and rebuild the cíties of Judah.
36   God's servants shall live there ánd possess it;
      the children of God's servants shall inherit it,
      and those who love God's name shall líve in it.   **R**

Psalm 70

R

1   Be pleased, O God, to delíver me!
      O Lord, make haste tó help me!
2   **Let them be put to shame and confusion**
      who séek my life!
      Let them be turned back and dishonored
      who desíre my pain!
3   Let them turn back because of their shame
      who say, "Ahá, Aha!
4   **May all who seek you**
      rejoice and be glád in you!
      May those who love your salvation
      say evermore, "Gód is great!"
5   **But I am poor and needy;**
      hasten to mé, O God!
      You are my help and my delíverer;
      O Lord, dó not tarry!   **R**

Psalm 71

R

1   In you, O Lord, do Í take refuge;
      let me never be pút to shame!
2   **In your righteousness deliver me and réscue me;**
      listen to me, and sáve me!
3   Be to me a rock of refuge,
      a strong fortress, to sáve me,
      for you are my rock ánd my fortress.
4   **Rescue me, O my God, from the hand óf the wicked,**
      from the grasp of the unjúst and cruel.

5 For you, O Lord, áre my hope,
   my trust, O Lord, fróm my youth.
6 **Upon you I have leaned from my birth;**
   it was you who took me from my móther's womb.
   My praise is contínually of you.   R

7 I have been an example to many,
   for you are mý strong refuge.
8 **My mouth is filled wíth your praise**
   and with your glory áll the day.
9 Do not cast me off in the time óf old age;
   do not forsake me when my stréngth is spent.
10 **For my enemies speak concérning me,**
    those who watch for my life consult togéther, saying,
11 **"Pursue and seize that person**
    whom God hás forsaken,
    for there is no delíverer."
12 O God, be not fár from me;
    O my God, make háste to help me!
13 Let my accusers be put to shame ánd consumed;
    let those who seek to hurt me
    be covered with scorn ánd disgrace.
14 **But I will hope contínually,**
    and will praise you yet móre and more.
15 My mouth will tell of your righteous acts,
    of your deeds of salvation áll day long,
    for their number is pást my knowledge.
16 **I will come praising the mighty deeds of thé Lord God,**
    I will praise your righteousness, yóurs alone.   R

17 O God, from my youth yóu have taught me,
    and I still proclaim your wóndrous deeds.
18 **So even to old age and gray hairs,**
    O God, do nót forsake me,
    until I proclaim your might
    to all the generátions to come.
19 Your power and your righteousness, O God,
    reach thé high heavens.
    You have done great things, O God;
    who ís like you?
20 **You, who have made me see many troubles and calamities,**
    will revive mé again;
    from the depths of the earth
    you will bring me úp again.
21 You will increase my honor,
    and comfort me ónce again.

22   I will also praise you with the harp
         for your faithfulness, Ó my God;
     I will sing praises to you wíth the lyre,
         O Holy One of Ísrael.
23   My lips will shout for joy,
         when I sing práises to you;
         my whole being also, which yóu have rescued.
24   All day long my tongue will speak of your ríghteous help,
         for those who tried to do me harm
         have been put to shame, ánd disgraced.   **R**

Psalm 72

R

1   Give the king your jústice, O God,
        and your righteousness to the róyal son!
2   May he judge your people with ríghteousness,
        and your póor with justice!
3   Let the mountains bear prosperity fór the people,
        and the hills, in ríghteousness!
4   **May he defend the cause of the poor óf the people,**
        give deliverance to the needy,
        and crush the oppréssor!
5   May he live while the sún endures,
        and as long as the moon, throughout all génerations!
6   **May he be like rain that falls on thé mown grass,**
        like showers that wáter the earth!
7   In his days may ríghteousness flourish,
        and peace abound, till the moon bé no more!
8   **May he have dominion from séa to sea,**
        and from the river to the ends óf the earth!   **R**

9   May his foes bow dówn before him,
        and his enemies líck the dust!
10 **May the kings of Tarshish and of the isles rénder him tribute,**
        may the kings of Sheba and Séba bring gifts!
11 May all kings fall down before him,
        all nátions serve him!
12 **For he delivers the needy when they call,**
        the poor and those who háve no helper.
13 He has pity on the weak ánd the needy,
        and saves the lives óf the needy.
14 **From oppression and violence he redéems their life;**
        and precious is their blood ín his sight.   **R**

15 Long may he live,
     may the gold of Sheba be gíven to him!
May prayer be made for him continually,
     and blessings invoked for him áll the day!
16 May there be abundance of grain ín the land;
     may it wave on the tops óf the mountains;
     may its fruit be like Lébanon;
and may they blossom forth in the cities
     like the grass óf the field!
17 **May his name endúre forever,**
     his fame continue as long ás the sun!
May people bless themsélves by him,
     all nations cáll him blessed!
18 Blessed be the Lord, the God of Ísrael,
     who alone does wóndrous things.
19 **Blessed be God's glorious náme forever;**
     may God's glory fill the whóle earth.
Amen ánd amen.
20 **The prayers of David, son of Jésse, are ended.**   **R**

Psalm 73

R

1 Truly God is good tó the upright,
     to those who are púre in heart.
2 **But as for me, my feet had álmost stumbled;**
     my steps had néarly slipped.
3 **For I was envious of the árrogant;**
     I saw the prosperity óf the wicked.
4 For they háve no pain;
     their bodies are sóund and sleek.
5 **They are not in trouble as óthers are;**
     they are not plagued like óther people.
6 Therefore pride ís their necklace;
     violence covers them líke a garment.
7 **Their eyes swell óut with fatness;**
     their hearts overflów with follies.
8 They mock and spéak with malice;
     arrogantly they thréaten oppression.
9 **They set their mouths agáinst heaven,**
     and their tongues range óver the earth.
10 Therefore the people túrn and praise them;
     and find no fáult in them.
11 **And they say, "How cán God know?**
     Is there knowledge in thé Most High?"

¹² Such áre the wicked;
always at ease, they incréase in riches.

¹³ **All in vain I have kept mý heart clean**
and washed my hands in ínnocence.

¹⁴ **For all day long I háve been plagued,**
and punished évery morning.   R

¹⁵ If I had said, "I will talk on ín this way,"
I would have been untrue to the circle óf your children.

¹⁶ But when I thought to understand this,
it seemed to me a wéarisome task,

¹⁷ until I went into the sanctuary of God;
then I percéived their end.

¹⁸ **Truly you set them in slippery places;**
you make them fáll to ruin.

¹⁹ How completely they áre destroyed!
How utterly swept away by terrors!

²⁰ **They are like a dream when óne awakes,**
on awakening you despíse their phantoms.   R

²¹ When my heart was embittered,
when I was wóunded within,

²² I was stupid and ignorant,
I was like a béast toward you.

²³ **Nevertheless I am continually with you;**
you hold mý right hand.

²⁴ **You guide me with counsel,**
and afterward you will receive mé with honor.

²⁵ Whom have I in héaven but you?
And there is nothing on earth that I desíre but you.

²⁶ **My flesh and my héart may fail,**
but God is the strength of my heart and my pórtion forever.

²⁷ Indeed, those who are far from yóu will perish;
you put an end to those who are fálse to you.

²⁸ **But for me it is good to bé near God;**
I have made the Lord God my refuge,
to tell of áll your works.   R

Psalm 74

R

¹ O God, why do you cast us óff forever?
Why do you burn with anger against the sheep óf your pasture?

² **Remember your congregation, which you acquired long ago,**
which you redeemed to be the tribe of your héritage!
Remember Mount Zion, where you cáme to live.

³ Direct your steps to the perpétual ruins;
     the enemy has destroyed everything in the sánctuary.
⁴ **Your foes have roared within your hóly place;**
     they set up their émblems there.
⁵ At the upper entrance they hacked
     the wooden tréllis with axes.
⁶ **And then, with hatchets and hammers,**
     they smashed all íts carved work.
⁷ They set your sanctuáry on fire;
     they desecrated the dwelling place of your name,
     bringing it tó the ground.
⁸ **They said to themselves, "We will utterly subdúe them;"**
     they burned all the meeting places of God ín the land.   **R**

⁹ We do not sée our emblems;
     there is no longer any prophet,
     and there is no one among us who knóws how long.
¹⁰ **How long, O God, is the fóe to mock?**
     Is the enemy to revile your náme forever?
¹¹ **Why do you hold báck your hand,**
     why do you keep your hand ín your bosom?
¹² Yet God my Ruler is fróm of old,
     working salvation ín the earth.
¹³ **You divided the sea bý your might;**
     you broke the heads of the dragons ín the waters.
¹⁴ You crushed the heads of Levíathan,
     you gave him as food for the creatures of the wílderness.
¹⁵ **You cut openings for spríngs and brooks;**
     you dried up ever-flówing streams.
¹⁶ Yours is the day, yours álso the night;
     you established the luminaries ánd the sun.
¹⁷ **You have fixed all the bounds óf the earth;**
     you made súmmer and winter.   **R**

¹⁸ Remember this, O Lord, how the énemy mocks,
     and an impious people revíles your name.
¹⁹ **Do not deliver the soul of your dove to the wild ánimals;**
     do not forget the life of your póor forever.
²⁰ Have regard for the cóvenant;
     for the dark places of the land are full of the haunts of víolence.
²¹ **Do not let the downtrodden be pút to shame;**
     let the poor and needy práise your name.
²² Rise up, O God, pléad your cause;
     remember how the impious mock you áll day long!
²³ **Do not forget the clamor óf your foes,**
     the uproar of your adversaries that goes up contínually!   **R**

Psalm 75

R

1   We give thanks to yóu, O God;
    we give thanks; your náme is near.
People tell of your wóndrous deeds.
2   At the set time that I appoint
    I will judge with équity.
3   **When the earth totters, and all its inhábitants,**
    it is I who keep its píllars steady.
4   I say to the boastful, "Dó not boast,"
    and to the wicked, "Do not lift úp your horn;
5   **do not lift up your hórn on high,**
    or speak with an ínsolent neck."   **R**

6   For not from the east or fróm the west
    and not from the wilderness comes lífting up;
7   **but it is God who execútes judgment,**
    putting down one and lifting úp another.
8   For in the hand of the Lord there is a cup,
    with foaming wíne, well mixed;
    and God will pour a draught from it,
        and all the wicked of the earth
        shall drain it tó the dregs.
9   **But I will rejóice forever,**
    I will sing praises to the Gód of Jacob.
10 **All the horns of the wicked I wíll cut off,**
    but the horns of the righteous shall bé exalted.   **R**

Psalm 76

R

1   In Judah Gód is known,
    whose name is great in Ísrael,
2   whose abode has been estáblished in Salem,
    whose dwelling place ís in Zion.
3   **There God broke the fláshing arrows,**
    the shield, the sword, and the wéapons of war.
4   You are glorious, more majestic
    than the everlásting mountains.
5   **The stouthearted were stripped of their spoil;**
    they sank ínto sleep;
    all the soldiers
        were unable to úse their hands.

⁶ At your rebuke, O God of Jacob,
    both rider and hórse lay stunned.   **R**

⁷ You are indeed tó be feared!
    Who can stand before you
    when once your ánger is roused?
⁸ **From the heavens you úttered judgment;**
    the earth feared ánd was still,
⁹ when God rose up to estáblish judgment,
    to save all the oppressed óf the earth.
¹⁰ **Even human wráth shall praise you;**
    you tie its residue aróund you.
¹¹ Make vows to the Lord your Gód, and keep them;
    let those who surround God bring gifts
    to the One tó be feared,
¹² **who cuts off the spírit of monarchs,**
    and makes the rulers of the éarth afraid.   **R**

Psalm 77

R

¹ I cry alóud to God,
    aloud to God, that Gód may hear me.
² **In the day of my trouble I séek the Lord;**
    in the night my hand is stretched out continually;
    my life refuses to be cómforted.
³ I think of God, ánd I moan;
    I meditate, and my spírit faints.
⁴ **You keep my éyelids from closing;**
    I am so troubled that I cánnot speak.
⁵ I consider the dáys of old,
    I remember the years lóng ago.
⁶ **I commune with my heart ín the night;**
    I meditate and séarch my spirit:
⁷ "Will the Lord spúrn forever
    and never again be fávorable?
⁸ **Has God's steadfast love céased forever?**
    Are God's promises at an end fór all time?
⁹ Has God forgotten tó be gracious?
    Has God's anger shut úp compassion?"
¹⁰ **And I say, "This ís my grief:**
    the right hand of the Most Hígh has changed."   **R**

11   I will call to mind the deeds óf the Lord;
       I will remember your wónders of old.
12   **I will meditate on áll your work,**
       and muse on your míghty deeds.
13   Your way, O Gód, is holy.
       What god is great líke our God?
14   You are the God whó works wonders,
       you manifested your might amóng the peoples.
15   **With your arm you redéemed your people,**
       the descendants of Jácob and Joseph.   **R**

16   When the waters saw yóu, O God,
       when the waters saw you, they were afraid,
       the very déeps trembled.
17   **The clouds póured out water;**
       the skies thundered;
       your arrows flashed on évery side.
18   The crash of your thunder was ín the whirlwind;
       your lightnings illumined the world;
       the earth trémbled and shook.
19   Your way was through the sea,
       your path through thé great waters;
       yet your footprints wére unseen.
20   **You led your people líke a flock**
       by the hand of Móses and Aaron.   **R**

Psalm 78

R

1   O my people, héar my teaching:
       listen to the words óf my mouth!
2   **I will open my mouth in a párable;**
       I will utter dark sayings fróm of old,
3   things that we have héard and known,
       that our ancestors háve told us.
4   **We will not hide them fróm their children,**
       but tell to the coming géneration
       the glorious deeds of the Lórd, the might,
       and wonders Gód has wrought.   **R**

5   The Lord established a testimóny in Jacob,
       and appointed a law in Ísrael.
       The Lord commanded our ancestors
       to téach their children
6   **that the next generation, the children**
       yet unborn, míght know them,

7   and might rise up and tell them tó their children,
      so that they should set their hópe in God,
  and not forgét God's works
      but keep Gód's commandments;

8   **and that they should not be like their áncestors,**
      a stubborn and rebellious géneration,
  a generation whose heart was nót steadfast,
      whose spirit was not fáithful to God.   **R**

9   The Ephramites, armed wíth the bow,
      turned back on the dáy of battle.

10   **They did not kéep God's covenant,**
      but refused to walk according tó God's law.

11   They forgot the deeds óf the Lord,
      the miracles that God had shówn them.

12   **The Lord wrought marvels in the sight of their áncestors**
      in the land of Egypt, in the fíelds of Zoan,

13   the Lord divided the sea and let them páss through it,
      and made the waters stand líke a heap,

14   **led them with a cloud ín the daytime,**
      and all night with a fíery light,

15   split rocks in the wílderness,
      and gave them drink abundantly as fróm the deep,

16   **made streams come out óf the rock,**
      and caused waters to flow dówn like rivers.   **R**

17   Yet they sinned still more agáinst God,
      rebelling against the Most High ín the desert.

18   They tested God ín their heart
      by demanding the fóod they craved.

19   They spoke agáinst God saying,
      "Can God spread a table in the wílderness?

20   **Even though God struck the rock so that water**
      gushed out and streams óverflowed,
      can God also give bread,
      or provide meat fór the people?"   **R**

21   The Lord heard and was fúll of rage,
      a fire was kindled agáinst Jacob;
      God's anger mounted against Ísrael,

22   because they had no faith in God,
      and did not trust God's sáving power.

23   **Yet the Lord commanded the skíes above,**
      opened the dóors of heaven,

24   **rained down on them manna to eat,**
      and gave them the gráin of heaven.

²⁵ Mortals ate the bread of angels;
  God sent them food ín abundance,
²⁶ caused the east wind to blow ín the heavens,
  and led out the south wínd in power.
²⁷ **God rained flesh down upon thém like dust,**
  winged birds like the sand óf the seas;
²⁸ God let them fall withín their camp,
  all aróund their dwellings.
²⁹ **And they ate and wére well filled,**
  for God gave them whát they craved.
³⁰ But before they had satisfíed their craving,
  while the food was still in their mouths,
³¹ the anger of God róse against them.
  God killed the stróngest of them,
  and laid low the flower of Ísrael.   R

³² In spite of all this théy still sinned;
  they did not believe ín these wonders.
³³ **So God made their days líke a breath,**
  turned their years ínto terror.
³⁴ Whenever God attacked them, they would lóok for God,
  repent and seek God éarnestly.
³⁵ **They remembered God wás their rock,**
  the Most High, théir redeemer,
³⁶ **whom they flattered wíth their mouths,**
  to whom they lied wíth their tongues.
³⁷ Their heart was not steadfast tóward God;
  they were not true to God's cóvenant.
³⁸ **Yet God, being compassionate,**
  forgave their iníquity,
  and did not destroy them,
  but restrained anger, and did not stír up wrath.   R

³⁹ God remembered that they wére but flesh,
  a wind that passes and does not cóme again.
⁴⁰ **How often they rebelled against God in the wílderness**
  and grieved God ín the desert!
⁴¹ They tested God again ánd again,
  and provoked the Holy One of Ísrael.
⁴² **They did not keep in mind God's power,**
  or the day when God redeemed them fróm the foe,
⁴³ **by displaying signs in Egypt**
  and miracles in the fíelds of Zoan.
⁴⁴ God turned their rívers to blood,
  so that they could not drink óf their streams,
⁴⁵ sent among them swarms of flies, which devóured them,

and frogs, whích destroyed them,
46 **gave their crops to the cáterpillar,**
and the fruit of their labor tó the locust,
47 **destroyed their vínes with hail,**
and their sycamóres with frost,
48 gave their cattle tó the hail,
and their flocks to thúnderbolts,
49 let loose on thém fierce anger,
rage, indignation, and distress,
a company of destróying angels.
50 **God made a path fór this anger,**
did not spare them from death,
but gave their lives óver to plague.
51 God struck all the first-bórn in Egypt,
the first issue of their strength in the ténts of Ham,
52 then led out the péople like sheep,
and guided them in the wilderness líke a flock.
53 **God led them in safety, so that they were nót afraid;**
but the sea overwhelmed their énemies.
54 And God brought them to the hóly hill,
to the mountains God's right hánd had won.
55 **God drove out nations befóre them,**
apportioned them for a possession,
and settled the tribes of Israel ín their tents.   R

56 Yet they tested and rebelled against the Móst High God,
whose testimonies they did nót observe.
57 **Rather they turned away and acted treacherously like their**
áncestors;
they twisted like a decéitful bow.
58 For they provoked God to anger with théir high places;
they moved God to jealousy wíth their idols.
59 **God heard, was full of wrath,**
and utterly rejected Ísrael.
60 God abandoned the dwelling at Shiloh,
the tent where God dwelled amóng mortals,
61 **and delivered divine power to captívity,**
divine glory to the hand óf the foe.
62 God gave the people of Israel tó the sword,
and vented wráth on them.
63 **Fire devoured théir young men,**
and their young women had no márriage song.
64 Their priests fell bý the sword,
and their widows made no lámentation.
65 **Then the Lord awoke ás from sleep,**
like a warrior shouting becáuse of wine.

66 The Lord put their adversáries to rout,
   put them to everlásting shame.
67 **God rejected the tént of Joseph,**
   and did not choose the tríbe of Ephraim,
68 **but chose the tríbe of Judah,**
   Mount Zion, whích God loves.
69 The Lord built the sanctuary like thé high heavens,
   like the earth which God has founded foréver.
70 **The Lord chose God's servant David,**
   and took him fróm the sheepfolds;
71 from tending the nursing ewes God brought him
   to be the shepherd of the people Jacob,
   of Israel, God's inhéritance.
72 **With upright heart God ténded them,**
   and guided them with skíllful hand.   **R**

Psalm 79

R

1 O God, the nations have come into your inhéritance;
   they have defiled your holy temple;
   they have made Jerusalém a ruin.
2 **They have given the bodies óf your servants**
   to the birds of the air for food,
   the flesh of your faithful to the wild animals óf the earth.
3 Those who surround Jerusalem have poured out
   their blóod like water;
   there was no one to búry them.
4 **We have become a taunt to our neighbors,**
   mocked and derided by thóse around us.
5 How long, O Lord? Will you be angry forever?
   Will your zeal búrn like fire?
6 Pour out your anger on the nations
   that do nót know you,
and on the kingdoms
   that do not call ón your name!
7 **For they have devóured Jacob,**
   and laid wáste his dwelling.   **R**

8 Do not remember against us the evils of our áncestors;
   let your compassion come speedily,
   for we are véry low.
9 Help us, O God of our salvation,
   for the glory óf your name;

deliver us, and forgive our sins,
  for yóur name's sake.
10 Why should the nations say,
    "Where ís their God?"
  Before our eyes let the avenging
    of your servants' spilled blood
    be known amóng the nations.
11 Let the groans of the prisoners cóme before you;
    according to your great power preserve those dóomed to die.
12 Return sevenfold into the bosom óf our neighbors
    the taunts with which they have taunted yóu, O Lord!
13 **Then we your people, the flock of your pasture,**
    will give thanks to yóu forever;
    from generation to generation we will recóunt your praise. R

Psalm 80

R

1 Listen, O Shepherd of Ísrael,
    you, who lead Joseph líke a flock!
    You, who are enthroned upon the chérubim,
2 shine forth before Ephraim, Benjamin ánd Manasseh.
    Stir up your might, and cóme to save us!
3 **Restore us, O God;**
    let your face shine, that we máy be saved!
4 O Lord God of hosts,
    how long will you be angry with your péople's prayers?
5 **You have fed them with the bread of tears,**
    and given them tears to drink ín full measure.
6 You make us the scorn óf our neighbors;
    and our enemies laugh amóng themselves.
7 **Restore us, O Gód of hosts;**
    let your face shine, that we máy be saved!   R

8 You brought a vine óut of Egypt;
    you drove out the nations and plánted it.
9 **You cleared the gróund for it;**
    it took deep root and fílled the land.
10 The mountains were covered wíth its shade,
    the mighty cedars wíth its branches;
11 **it sent out its branches tó the sea,**
    and its shoots tó the river.
12 Why then have you broken dówn its walls,
    so that all who pass along the way plúck its fruit?
13 **The boar from the forest rávages it,**
    and all that move in the field féed on it.   R

¹⁴ Turn again, O God of hosts!
  look down from héaven and see:
  have regard for this vine,
¹⁵   **the stock which your ríght hand planted.**
¹⁶ They have burned it with fire, they have cút it down;
  may they perish at the rebuke of your cóuntenance!
¹⁷ **But let your hand be upon those of yóur right hand,**
  the ones whom you have made strong fór yourself!
¹⁸ Then we will never turn báck from you;
  give us life, and we will call ón your name!
¹⁹ **Restore us, O Lord Gód of hosts!**
  let your face shine, that we máy be saved! **R**

Psalm 81

R

¹ Sing aloud to Gód our strength;
  shout for joy to the Gód of Jacob!
² **Raise a song, sound the támbourine,**
  the sweet lyre wíth the harp.
³ Blow the trumpet at thé new moon,
  at the full moon, on óur feast day.
⁴ **For it is a statute for Ísrael,**
  an ordinance of the Gód of Jacob,
⁵ **who made it a decrée in Joseph,**
  when God went out against the lánd of Egypt. **R**

I hear a voice I dó not know:
⁶ **"I relieved your shoulder of the burden;**
  your hands were freed fróm the basket.
⁷ In distress you called, and I delívered you;
  I answered you in the secret place of thunder;
  I tested you at the waters of Méribah.
⁸ **Hear, O my people, while I admónish you!**
  O Israel, if you would but lísten to me!
⁹ There shall be no strange gód among you;
  you shall not bow down to a fóreign god.
¹⁰ **I am the Lord your God,**
  who brought you up out of the lánd of Egypt.
  Open wide your mouth, and Í will fill it!" **R**

¹¹ "But my people did not listen tó my voice;
  Israel would not submít to me.
¹² **So I gave them over to their stúbborn hearts,**
  to follow théir own counsels.

13   O that my people would lísten to me,
        that Israel would walk ín my ways!
14   **Then I would quickly subdue their énemies,**
        and turn my hand agáinst their foes.
15   Those who hate the Lord dený the Lord,
        and their fate is séaled forever.
16   **But I would feed you with the finest óf the wheat,**
        and with honey from the rock I would sátisfy you."   **R**

Psalm 82

R

1   God is seated in the divíne council,
        and in the midst of the góds holds judgment:
2   **"How long will you júdge unjustly**
        and show partiality tó the wicked?
3   Give justice to the weak ánd the orphan;
        maintain the right of the afflicted and the déstitute.
4   **Rescue the weak ánd the needy;**
        deliver them from the hand óf the wicked."
5   They have neither knowledge nor understanding,
        they walk abóut in darkness;
        all the foundations of the éarth are shaken.
6   **I said, "You are gods,**
        godlike offspring, áll of you;
7   nevertheless you shall die like mortals,
        and fall like ány noble."
8   **Arise, O God, júdge the earth,**
        for to you belong áll the nations!   **R**

Psalm 83

R

1   O God, do nót keep silence;
        do not be silent or stíll, O God!
2   **Even now your enemies áre in tumult;**
        those who hate you have ráised their heads.
3   They lay crafty plans agáinst your people;
        they consult together against those yóu protect.
4   They say, "Come, let us wipe them out ás a nation;
        let the name of Israel be remémbered no more!"
5   **They conspire with óne accord;**
        against you they make a cóvenant—

⁶ the tents of Edom and the Íshmaelites,
    Moab and thé Hagrites,
⁷ Gebal and Ammon and Ámalek,
    Philistia with the inhabitánts of Tyre;
⁸ Assyria also hás joined them;
    they are the strong arm of the chíldren of Lot.   **R**

⁹ Do to them as you did to Mídian,
    as to Sisera and Jabin at the Wádi Kishon,
¹⁰ **who were destróyed at Endor,**
    who became dung fór the ground.
¹¹ Make their nobles like Óreb and Zeeb,
    all their leaders like Zebah and Zálmunna,
¹² **who said, "Let us take the pastures of God**
    for our ówn possession."
¹³ O my God, make them like whirling dust,
    like chaff befóre the wind.   **R**

¹⁴ As fire consumes the forest,
    as the flame sets the móuntains ablaze,
¹⁵ so pursue them with your tempest
    and terrify them with yóur whirlwind!
¹⁶ **Fill their fáces with shame,**
    so that they seek your náme, O Lord.
¹⁷ Let them be put to shame and dismayed forever;
    let them perish ín disgrace.
¹⁸ **Let them know that you alone,**
    whose name is the Lord,
    are the Most High over áll the earth.   **R**

Psalm 84

R

¹ How lovely is your dwélling place,
    O Lórd of hosts!
² **My soul longs, indeed it faints**
    for the courts óf the Lord;
    my heart and flesh sing for joy
    to the líving God.
³ O Lord of hosts, my Ruler ánd my God,
    at your altars even the sparrow fínds a home,
    and the swallow a nest fór herself,
    where she may láy her young.
⁴ **Blessed are those who dwell ín your house,**
    ever sínging your praise!

⁵ Blessed are those whose strength ís in you,
    in whose heart are the híghways to Zion.
⁶ **As they go through the valley of tears,**
    they make it a pláce of springs;
    the early rain also covers ít with pools.   R

⁷ They go from stréngth to strength;
    the God of gods will be séen in Zion.
⁸ **O Lord God of hosts, héar my prayer;**
    O God of Jácob, hear!
⁹ **Behold our shíeld, O God;**
    look upon the face of yóur anointed!
¹⁰ For a day in your courts is better
    than a thóusand elsewhere.
    I would rather be a doorkeeper in the house of my God
    than dwell in the tents of wíckedness.
¹¹ For the Lord God is a sun ánd a shield,
    and bestows fávor and honor.
    The Lord witholds no good thing
    from those who walk úprightly.
¹² **O Lord of hosts,**
    blessed are they who trúst in you!   R

Psalm 85

R

¹ Lord, you showed favor tó your land;
    you restored the fórtunes of Jacob.
² **You forgave the iniquity óf your people;**
    you pardoned áll their sin.
³ You withdrew áll your wrath;
    you turned from yóur hot anger.
⁴ **Restore us again, O God of óur salvation,**
    and put away your indignation tóward us!
⁵ Will you be angry with ús forever?
    Will you prolong your anger to all génerations?
⁶ Will you not revive ús again,
    that your people may rejóice in you?
⁷ **Show us your steadfast lóve, O Lord,**
    and grant us yóur salvation.   R

⁸ Let me hear what God the Lord will speak,
    for God will speak peace tó the people,
    to the faithful, to those who turn to God ín their hearts.

⁹ Surely salvation is at hand for those who féar the Lord,
    that glory may dwell ín our land.
¹⁰ Steadfast love and faithfulnéss will meet;
    righteousness and peace will kíss each other.
¹¹ **Faithfulness will spring up fróm the ground,**
    and righteousness will look down fróm the sky.
¹² The Lord will give whát is good,
    and our land will yíeld its increase.
¹³ **Righteousness will go befóre the Lord,**
    and make a path for Gód's footsteps.   **R**

Psalm 86

R

¹ Hear, O Lord, and ánswer me,
    for I am póor and needy.
² **Preserve my life, for I am devóted to you;**
    save your servant who trústs in you.
  You are my God;
³   be gracious to mé, O Lord,
    for I cry to you áll day long.
⁴ **Gladden the life óf your servant,**
    for I lift up my life to yóu, O Lord.
⁵ For you, O Lord, are good ánd forgiving,
    abounding in steadfast love to all who cáll on you.
⁶ **O Lord, héar my prayer;**
    listen to my cry of súpplication.
⁷ In the day of my trouble I cáll on you,
    for you will ánswer me.   **R**

⁸ There is none like you among the góds, O Lord,
    nor are there any wórks like yours.
⁹ **All the nations you have made shall come**
    and bow down before yóu, O Lord,
    and shall glorifý your name.
¹⁰ For you are great and do wóndrous things,
    you alóne are God.
¹¹ **Teach me your way, O Lord,**
    that I may walk ín your truth;
    give me an undivided heart to revére your name.
¹² I give thanks to you, O Lord my God, with mý whole heart,
    and I will glorify your náme forever.
¹³ **For great is your steadfast lóve toward me;**
    you have delivered my life from the dépths of Sheol.   **R**

14 O God, the insolent rise úp against me;
          a ruthless band seeks my life,
          and they do not set yóu before them.
15 **But you, O Lord, are a merciful and grácious God,**
          slow to anger and abounding in steadfast love and
              fáithfulness.
16 Turn to me ánd be gracious;
          give your strength to your servant;
          save the child of yóur maidservant.
17 **Show me a good sign,**
          so that those who hate me may see it ánd be shamed.
          Surely you, Lord, have helped and cómforted me. 　**R**

Psalm 87

R

1 On the holy mountains God fóunded it;
2 the Lord loves the gates of Zion
          more than all the dwéllings of Jacob.
3 **Glorious things are spóken of you,**
          O cíty of God.
4 Among those who know me I remember Rahab and Babylon;
          Philistia too, and Tyre, with Ethiópia—
          "**This one was born thére**," **they say.**
5 And of Zion it shall be said,
          "**This one and that one were bórn there**";
          for the Most High will estáblish it.
6 The Lord records and registers the peoples:
          "**This one was bórn there.**"
7 "**All who suffered among you will síng and dance.**" 　**R**

Psalm 88

R

1 O Lord, God of mý salvation,
          by day I cry out, by night I ám before you.
2 **Let my prayer cóme to you;**
          listen tó my cry.
3 For my soul is fúll of troubles,
          and my life draws néar to Sheol.
4 **I am counted among those who go down tó the Pit;**
          I am like those who háve no help,
5 like those forsaken amóng the dead,
          like the slain that lie ín the grave,
          like those whom you remémber no more,
          for they are cut off fróm your hand.

6   You have put me in the depths óf the Pit,
        in the regions dárk and deep.
7   **Your anger lies heavy upón me,**
        and you overwhelm me with áll your waves.   **R**

8   You have caused my companions to shun me;
        you have made me a thing of hórror to them.
    I am shut in so that I cannot escape;
        my eye grows dím through sorrow.
9   Every day I call on yóu, O Lord;
        I spread out my hánds to you.
10 **Do you work wonders fór the dead?**
        Do the shades rise úp to praise you?
11 Is your steadfast love declared ín the grave,
        or your faithfulness ín Abaddon?
12 **Are your wonders known ín the darkness,**
        or your saving help in the land of forgétfulness?   **R**

13 But I cry to yóu, O Lord;
        in the morning my prayer cómes before you.
14 **O Lord, why do you cást me off?**
        Why do you hide your fáce from me?
15 Wretched and close to death fróm my youth
        I suffer your terrors; I am désperate.
16 **Your anger has swept óver me;**
        your dread assáults destroy me.
17 They surround me like a flood áll day long;
        from all sides they close ín on me.
18 **You have caused friend and neighbor to shún me;**
        my companions áre in darkness.   **R**

Psalm 89

R

1   I will sing of your steadfast love, O Lórd, forever,
        with my mouth I will proclaim your faithfulness to all
            génerations.
2   **Your steadfast love is established foréver,**
        your faithfulness is firm ás the heavens.
3   You have said, "I have made a covenant with my chósen one,
        I have sworn to Dávid my servant:
4   **'I will establish your descendants foréver,**
        and build your throne for all génerations.'"   **R**

⁵ Let the heavens praise your wónders, O Lord,
  your faithfulness in the assembly of the hóly ones.
⁶ **For who in the skies can be compared tó the Lord?**
  Who among the heavenly beings is líke the Lord,
⁷ **a God feared in the council of the hóly ones,**
  great and awesome above all whó are present?
⁸ O Lord God of hosts,
  who is as mighty as you áre, O Lord?
  Your faithfulness surróunds you.
⁹ **You rule the raging óf the sea;**
  when its waves ríse, you still them.
¹⁰ You crushed Rahab líke a carcass,
  you scattered your enemies with your míghty arm.
¹¹ **The heavens are yours, the earth álso is yours;**
  the world and all that is in it—you have fóunded them.
¹² The north and the south—you creáted them;
  Tabor and Hermon joyously práise your name.
¹³ **You have a míghty arm;**
  strong is your hand, high yóur right hand.   **R**

¹⁴ Righteousness and justice are the foundation óf your throne;
  steadfast love and faithfulness gó before you.
¹⁵ **Happy are the people who know the féstal shout,**
  who walk, O Lord, in the light of your cóuntenance.
¹⁶ **who rejoice in your name áll day long,**
  and extol your ríghteousness.
¹⁷ For you are the glory óf their strength;
  by your favor our horn ís exalted.
¹⁸ **For our shield belongs tó the Lord,**
  our king to the Holy One of Ísrael.
¹⁹ Then you spoke in a vision to your faithful óne, and said:
  "I have set the crown upon one who is mighty,
  I have exalted one chosen fróm the people.
²⁰ I have found Dávid, my servant;
  with my holy oil I have anóinted him;
²¹ **so that my hand shall bé with him,**
  my arm also shall stréngthen him.
²² The enemy shall nót outwit him,
  the wicked shall not húmble him.
²³ **I will crush his foes befóre him**
  and strike down those whó hate him.
²⁴ My faithfulness and my steadfast love shall bé with him,
  and in my name his horn shall bé exalted.
²⁵ **I will set his hand ón the sea**
  and his right hand ón the rivers.

26 He shall cry to me, 'You áre my Father,
      my God, and the Rock of mý salvation.'
27 **And I will make him thé first-born,**
      the highest of the kings óf the earth.
28 My steadfast love I will keep for hím forever,
      and my covenant will stand fírm for him.
29 **I will establish his líne forever**
      and his throne as long as the héavens endure.   **R**

30 "If his children forsáke my law
      and do not walk according to my órdinances,
31 **if they violáte my statutes**
      and do not keep mý commandments,
32 then I will punish their transgression wíth the rod
      and their iníquity with plagues;
33 **but I will not remove my steadfast lóve from him,**
      or be false to my fáithfulness.
34 I will not violate my cóvenant,
      or alter the word that went forth fróm my lips.
35 **Once for all I have sworn by my hóliness;**
      I will not líe to David.
36 His line shall contínue forever,
      his throne shall endure before me líke the sun.
37 **Like the moon it shall be estáblished forever;**
      it shall stand firm while the skíes endure."   **R**

38 But now you have spurned and rejécted him;
      you are full of anger against yóur anointed.
39 **You have renounced the covenant wíth your servant;**
      you have defiled his crown ín the dust.
40 You have broken through áll his walls;
      you have laid his stronghólds in ruins.
41 **All that pass by plúnder him;**
      he has become the scorn óf his neighbors.
42 You have exalted the right hand óf his foes;
      you have made all his enemíes rejoice.
43 **Moreover, you have turned back the edge óf his sword,**
      and you have not supported hím in battle.
44 You have removed the scepter fróm his hand,
      and hurled his throne tó the ground.
45 **You have cut short the days óf his youth;**
      you have covered hím with shame.   **R**

46 How long, O Lord? Will you hide yoursélf forever?
      How long will your anger búrn like fire?

47 Remember how short mý life is—
    you have created such emptiness fór all mortals!
48 Who can live and néver see death?
    Who can escape the pówer of Sheol?
49 Lord, where is your steadfast lóve of old,
    which by your faithfulness you swóre to David?
50 Remember, O Lord, how your sérvant is taunted;
    how I bear in my bosom the insults óf the peoples,
51 with which your enemies táunt, O Lord,
    with which they taunted the footsteps of yóur anointed.
52 Blessed be the Lórd forever!
    Amen ánd amen.   R

Psalm 90

R

1 Lord, you have been our dwelling place
    in all génerations.
2 Before the mountains were brought forth,
    or ever you had formed the earth and the world,
    from everlasting to everlasting yóu are God.
3 You turn us back tó the dust,
    and say, "Turn báck, you mortals!"
4 For a thousand years in your sight
    are as yesterday when ít is past,
    or as a watch ín the night.
5 You sweep them away; they are líke a dream,
    like grass which is renewed ín the morning:
6 in the morning it flourishes and ís renewed;
    in the evening it fádes and withers.   R

7 For we are consumed bý your anger;
    by your wrath we are óverwhelmed.
8 You have set our iniquities befóre you,
    our secret sins in the light of your cóuntenance.
9 For all our days pass away únder your wrath,
    our years come to an end líke a sigh.
10 The years of our life are threescóre and ten,
    or if we are stróng fourscore;
    yet their span is but tóil and trouble;
    they are soon gone, and we flý away.
11 Who considers the power of your anger,
    the awesomeness óf your wrath?
12 So teach us to number our days
    that we may receive a héart of wisdom.   R

13   Turn, O Lórd! How long?
        Have compassion ón your servants!
14   **Satisfy us in the morning with your stéadfast love,**
        that we may rejoice and be glad áll our days.
15   Make us glad as many days as you have afflícted us,
        and as many years as we háve seen evil.
16   **Let your work be manifest tó your servants,**
        and your glorious power tó their children.
17   **Let the favor of the Lord our God be upon us,**
        and establish the work óf our hands;
        yes, establish the work óf our hands.   **R**

Psalm 91

R

1   Those who dwell in the shelter of thé Most High,
        who abide in the shadow of the Almighty,
2   will say tó the Lord,
    "My refuge ánd my fortress;
        my God, in whóm I trust."
3   For the Lord will deliver you from the snáre of the fowler
        and from the deadly péstilence
4   and will cover yóu with pinions;
        under the Lord's wings you wíll find refuge.
        God's faithfulness is a shíeld and buckler.
5   You will not fear the terror óf the night,
        nor the arrow that flíes by day,
6   **nor the pestilence that stálks in darkness,**
        nor the destruction that wástes at noonday.
7   A thousand may fall at your side,
        ten thousand at yóur right hand,
        but it will not cóme near you.
8   **You will look only wíth your eyes**
        and see the end óf the wicked.
9   Because you have made the Lórd your refuge,
        the Most High your hábitation,
10   **no evil sháll befall you,**
        no plague come néar your tent.   **R**

11   For God will give angels charge óver you
        to guard you in áll your ways.
12   **They will bear you up ón their hands**
        lest you dash your foot agáinst a stone.
13   You will tread on the lion ánd the adder,
        the young lion and the serpent you will trample únder foot.

14 Those who cling to me in love I wíll deliver;
    I will protect them, because they knów my name.
15 When they call me, I will ánswer them;
    I will be with them in trouble,
    I will rescue them and hónor them.
16 I will satisfy them wíth long life
    and show them mý salvation.   R

Psalm 92

R

1 It is good to give thanks tó the Lord,
    to sing praises to your name, Ó Most High;
2 to declare your steadfast love ín the morning,
    and your faithfulnéss by night,
3 to the music of the lute ánd the harp,
    to the melody óf the lyre.
4 For you, O Lord, have made me glad bý your work;
    at the works of your hands I síng for joy.
5 How great are your wórks, O Lord!
    Your thoughts are véry deep!
6 The senseless cánnot know,
    the foolish cannot únderstand this:
7 though the wicked spróut like grass
    and all evildóers flourish,
    they are doomed to destrúction forever,
8 but you, O Lord, are on hígh forever.
9 For your enemies, O Lord,
    for your enemies shall pérish;
    all evildoers sháll be scattered.   R

10 But you have exalted my horn like that of thé wild ox;
    you have poured over mé fresh oil.
11 My eyes have seen the downfall óf my enemies,
    my ears have heard the doom of my évil assailants.
12 The righteous flourish líke the palm tree,
    and grow like a cedar in Lébanon.
13 They are planted in the house óf the Lord,
    they flourish in the courts óf our God.
14 Still productive in old age,
    they are full of sap and green,
15 showing that the Lord ís upright.
    The Lord is my rock in whom there is no
      unríghteousness.   R

Psalm 93

R

1 The Lord reigns and is robed in májuśty;
   the Lord is robed and is gírded with strength.
   The Lord has estáblished the world;
   it shall néver be moved.
2 Your throne has been established fróm of old;
   you are from éverlasting!
3 **The floods have lifted up, O Lord,**
   the floods have lifted úp their voice,
   the floods lift úp their roaring.
4 Mightier than the thunders of mány waters,
   mightier than the waves of the sea,
   the Lord on hígh is mighty!
5 **Your decrees are véry sure;**
   holiness befits your house,
   O Lord, for évermore.   R

Psalm 94

R

1 O Lord, Gód of vengeance,
   God of vengéance, shine forth!
2 **Rise up, O judge óf the earth;**
   give to the proud what théy deserve!
3 O Lord, how long sháll the wicked,
   how long shall the wícked triumph?
4 **They pour out their árrogant words;**
   all the evildóers boast.
5 They crush your péople, O Lord,
   and afflict your héritage.
6 **They kill the widow ánd the stranger,**
   they múrder the orphan,
7 **and they say, "The Lord dóes not see;**
   the God of Jacob does nót perceive."
8 Understand, you stúpid people!
   Fools, when will yóu be wise?
9 **Does not God, who created the éar, hear?**
   Does not God, who formed the éye, see?
10 Does not God, who disciplines nations
    and teaches knowledge to húmankind,
        punish?
11 **The Lord knows our thoughts,**
    that they are but an émpty breath.   R

¹² Blessed are those whom you discipline, Ó Lord,
and whom you teach fróm your law,
¹³ giving them respite from dáys of trouble,
until a pit is dug fór the wicked.
¹⁴ **For the Lord will not forsáke God's people,**
and will not abandon this héritage;
¹⁵ **for justice will return tó the righteous,**
and all the upright in heart will fóllow it.
¹⁶ Who rises up for me agáinst the wicked?
Who stands up for me against évildoers?
¹⁷ If the Lord had not béen my help,
soon I would have dwelled in the lánd of silence.
¹⁸ **When I thought, "Mý foot slips,"**
your steadfast love, O Lord, héld me up.
¹⁹ When the cares of my héart are many,
your consolations chéer my soul.
²⁰ **Can wicked rulers be allíed with you,**
those who frame míschief by statute?
²¹ They band together against the life óf the righteous,
and condemn the innocent tó death.
²² **But the Lord has becóme my stronghold,**
and my God the rock óf my refuge.
²³ God will turn their iniquity against them
and destroy them for their wíckedness;
the Lord our God wíll destroy them.   R

Psalm 95

R

¹ O come, let us sing tó the Lord;
let us make a joyful noise to the rock of óur salvation!
² Let us come into God's presence wíth thanksgiving;
let us make a joyful noise with sóngs of praise!
³ For the Lord is a gréat God,
and a great Ruler abóve all gods,
⁴ in whose hands are the depths óf the earth
and also the heights óf the mountains.
⁵ **The sea belongs to Gód who made it,**
and the dry land, becáuse God formed it.   R

⁶ O come, let us worship ánd bow down,
let us kneel before the Lórd, our Maker!
⁷ For the Lord ís our God,
we are the people of God's pasture,
the sheep óf God's hand.

Hear the voice of the Lórd today!
8   Harden not your hearts, as at Meribah,
        as on the day at Massah in the wílderness,
9   when your ancestors tésted me,
        and put me to the proof, though they had séen my work.
10   **For forty years I loathed that géneration**
        and said, "They are a people whose hearts go astray,
        and they do not knów my ways."
11   **Therefore I swore ín my anger,**
        "They shall not énter my rest."   **R**

Psalm 96

R

1   O sing to the Lord á new song;
        sing to the Lord, áll the earth!
2   **Sing to the Lord, bléss God's name;**
        proclaim God's salvation from dáy to day.
3   Declare the Lord's glory amóng the nations,
        the Lord's marvelous works among áll the peoples!
4   **For great is the Lord and greatly tó be praised,**
        to be feared abóve all gods.
5   For all the gods of the péoples are idols;
        but the Lord máde the heavens.
6   **Honor and majesty are befóre the Lord**
        in whose sanctuary are stréngth and beauty.   **R**

7   Ascribe to the Lord, O families óf the peoples,
        ascribe to the Lord glóry and strength!
8   **Ascribe to the Lord a glórious name!**
        Bring an offering, and come into the courts
        óf the Lord!
9   Worship the Lord in hóly splendor;
        tremble before the Lord, áll the earth!
10   Say among the nations, "The Lord reigns!
        The Lord has established the world, it shall néver be moved.
        The Lord will judge the people with équity."
11   Let the heavens be glad, and let the éarth rejoice;
        let the sea roar, and all that fills it;
12   let the field rejoice, and éverything in it!
    Then shall all the trees of the wood sing for joy befóre the Lord,
13   **who comes to júdge the earth.**
        The Lord will judge the world with ríghteousness,
        and the péoples with truth.   **R**

Psalm 97

R

1 The Lord reigns; let the éarth rejoice;
 let the many coastlánds be glad!
2 **Clouds and thick darkness surróund the Lord;**
 righteousness and justice are the foundation
 óf God's throne.
3 Fire goes befóre the Lord,
 and burns up God's adversaries on évery side.
4 **The Lord's lightnings illúmine the world;**
 the earth sées and trembles.
5 The mountains melt like wax befóre the Lord,
 before the Lord of áll the earth.
6 **The heavens proclaim God's ríghteousness**
 and all the peoples behóld God's glory.   R

7 All worshipers of images are put to shame,
 who make their boast in wórthless idols;
 all gods bow down befóre the Lord.
8 **Zion hears ánd is glad,**
 and the daughters of Judah rejoice,
 because of your júdgments, O God.
9 For you, O Lord, are most high over áll the earth;
 you are exalted far abóve all gods.
10 **The Lord loves those who háte evil,**
 preserves the lives of the faithful,
 and delivers them from the hand óf the wicked.
11 Light dawns fór the righteous,
 and joy for the upríght in heart.
12 **Rejoice in the Lord, Ó you righteous,**
 and give thanks to God's hóly name!   R

Psalm 98

R

1 O sing to the Lord á new song,
 for the Lord has done márvelous things!
 God's right hand and hóly arm
 have gótten the victory.
2 **The Lord has declared víctory,**
 and has revealed vindication in the sight óf the nations.

³ The Lord has remembered steadfast love and faithfulness
    to the house of Ísrael.
  All the ends of the earth have seen
      the victory óf our God.   R

⁴ Make a joyful noise to the Lord, áll the earth;
      break forth into joyous song ánd sing praises!
⁵ Sing praises to the Lord wíth the lyre,
      with the lyre and the sound of mélody!
⁶ **With trumpets and the sound óf the horn**
      make a joyful noise before the Rúler, the Lord!   R

⁷ Let the sea roar, and áll that fills it;
      the world and those who dwéll in it!
⁸ **Let the floods cláp their hands;**
      let the hills sing for joy together befóre the Lord,
⁹ **who comes to júdge the earth.**
  The Lord will judge the world with ríghteousness,
      and the peoples with équity.   R

Psalm 99

R

¹ The Lord reigns; let the péoples tremble!
      The Lord sits enthroned upon the cherubim;
      let the éarth quake!
² **The Lord is gréat in Zion;**
      and is exalted over áll the peoples.
³ Let them praise your great and wóndrous name.
      Holy ís the Lord!
⁴ Mighty Ruler, lover of justice,
      you have established équity;
  you have executed justice
      and righteousnéss in Jacob.
⁵ Extol the Lord our God;
      worship at the Lórd's footstool.
  Holy ís the Lord!   R

⁶ Moses and Aaron were amóng God's priests,
      Samuel also was among those who called ón God's name.
  They cried to the Lord, who ánswered them,
⁷   **who spoke to them in the píllar of cloud.**
  They kept God's téstimonies,
      and the statutes Gód gave them.

⁸ **O Lord, our God, you ánswered them;**
 you were a forgiving God to them,
 but an avenger of théir wrongdoings.
⁹ Extol the Lord our God,
 and worship at the hóly mountain.
 Surely the Lord our Gód is holy! **R**

Psalm 100

R

¹ Make a joyful noise to the Lord, áll the lands!
² **Serve the Lord with gladness!**
 Come into God's présence with singing!
³ Know that the Lord, who made ús, is God.
 We are the Lord's;
 we are the people of God,
 the sheep óf God's pasture.
⁴ Enter God's gates with thanksgiving,
 and God's cóurts with praise!
 Give thanks and bléss God's name!
⁵ For the Lórd is good;
 God's steadfast love endures for ever,
 God's faithfulness to all génerations. **R**

Psalm 101

R

¹ I will sing of loyalty and jústice;
 I will sing to yóu, O Lord.
² **I will study the blámeless way.**
 When shall Í grasp it?
 I will walk with integrity of heart
 withín my house;
³ **I will not set before my eyes**
 anything thát is wicked.
 I hate the work of those who fáll away;
 it shall be no párt of me.
⁴ **A perverse heart shall be fár from me;**
 I will know nóthing of evil.
⁵ One who secretly slanders a neighbor
 I wíll destroy.
 A conceited look and an arrogant heart
 I will not tólerate.

6   I will look with favor on the faithful ín the land,
          so that they may líve with me;
      whoever walks in the blámeless way
          shall minister tó me.

7   No one who practices deceit shall remain ín my house;
          no one who utters lies
          shall continue ín my presence.

8   **Morning by morning I will destroy**
          all the wicked ín the land,
      cutting off all evildoers
          from the city óf the Lord.   R

Psalm 102

R

1   Hear my práyer, O Lord;
          let my cry cóme to you!

2   **Do not hide your fáce from me**
          in the day of mý distress!
      Lísten to me;
          answer me speedily in the day whén I call!

3   For my days pass away like smoke,
          and my bones burn líke a furnace.

4   **my heart is withered like dried up grass;**
          I am too wasted to éat my bread.

5   Because of my loud groaning
          my bones cling tó my flesh.

6   **I am like an owl of the wilderness,**
          like a little owl of thé waste places;

7   I lie awake,
          I am like a lonely bird ón a housetop.

8   **All day long my enemies taunt me,**
          those who deride me use my name fór a curse.

9   For I eat áshes like bread,
          and mingle tears wíth my drink,

10   because of your indignátion and anger;
          for you have lifted me up and thrown mé away.

11   **My days are like an évening shadow;**
          I wíther like grass.   R

12   But you, O Lord, are enthróned forever;
          your name endures to all génerations.

13   **You will arise and have píty on Zion;**
          it is the time to favor it;
          the appointed tíme has come.

14 For your servants hold íts stones dear,
   and have pity ón its dust.
15 **The nations will fear the name óf the Lord,**
   and all the kings of the éarth your glory.
16 For the Lord will búild up Zion,
   and gloriously wíll appear;
17 **the Lord will turn toward the prayer of the déstitute,**
   and will not despíse their prayer.
18 Let this be recorded for a generátion to come,
   so that a people yet unborn may práise the Lord:
19 **that the Lord looked down from a hóly height,**
   from heaven the Lord looked át the earth,
20 **to hear the groans of the prísoners,**
   to set free those who were dóomed to die;
21 **that the name of the Lord may be declared in Zion,**
   and God's praise in Jerúsalem,
22 **when peoples and kingdoms gather together to wórship the Lord. R**

23 The Lord has broken my strength ín mid-course,
   and has shórtened my days.
24 **"Oh my God," I say, "do not take me away**
   in the midst óf my days,
   you whose years endure
   throughout all the génerations!"
25 Long ago you laid the foundation óf the earth,
   and the heavens are the work óf your hands.
26 **They will perish, but yóu endure;**
   they will all wear out líke a garment.
   You change them like clothing, and they páss away;
27 but you are the same, and your years háve no end.
28 **The children of your servants shall dwéll secure;**
   their posterity shall be estáblished before you.   R

Psalm 103

R

1 Bless the Lord, Ó my soul!
   and all that is within me,
   bless God's hóly name!
2 **Bless the Lord, Ó my soul,**
   and forget not all God's bénefits,
3 who forgives all your iníquity,
   who heals all yóur diseases,
4 **who redeems your life fróm the pit,**
   who crowns you with steadfast lóve and mercy,
5 **who satisfies you with good as long ás you live**
   so that your youth is renewed líke the eagle's.   R

⁶ The Lord, who works víndication
    and justice for all who áre oppressed,
⁷ has made known God's wáys to Moses,
    God's acts to the people of Ísrael.
⁸ **The Lord is merciful and grácious,**
    slow to anger and abounding in stéadfast love.
⁹ The Lord will not alwáys contend,
    nor nourish ánger forever.
¹⁰ **The Lord does not deal with us according tó our sins,**
    nor repay us according to our iníquities.
¹¹ For as the heavens are high abóve the earth,
    so great is the Lord's steadfast love toward those
    whó are faithful;
¹² **as far as the east is fróm the west,**
    so far the Lord removes our transgréssions from us.
¹³ As a father shows compassion tó his children,
    so the Lord shows compassion tó the faithful.
¹⁴ **For the Lord knóws our frame,**
    and remembers that wé are dust.   **R**

¹⁵ As for mortals, their days áre like grass;
    they flourish like a flower óf the field;
¹⁶ the wind passes over it, and ít is gone,
    and the field knows the flówer no more.
¹⁷ **But the steadfast love óf the Lord**
    is from everlasting to éverlasting
    upon those whó are faithful,
    and the Lord's righteousness to chíldren's children,
¹⁸ **to those who keep God's cóvenant**
    and remember to do Gód's commandments.
¹⁹ The Lord has established a throne ín the heavens,
    and God's kingdom rules óver all.
²⁰ **Bless the Lórd, O angels,**
    you mighty ones who do God's bidding,
    obedient tó God's word.
²¹ Bless the Lord, áll the hosts,
    the ministers that dó God's will.
²² **Bless the Lord, all God's works,**
    in all places of Gód's dominion.
    Bless the Lord, Ó my soul!   **R**

Psalm 104

R

¹ Bless the Lord, Ó my soul!
   O Lord my God, you are véry great!
   You are clothed with honor and májesty,
² and wrapped in light as wíth a garment;
   you stretch out the heavens líke a tent,
³ **and lay the beams of your chambers ón the waters;**
   you make the clouds your cháriot,
   and ride on the wings óf the wind;
⁴ **you make the winds your méssengers,**
   fire and flame your mínisters.
⁵ You set the earth on íts foundations,
   so that it shall néver be shaken.
⁶ **You covered it with the deep as wíth a garment;**
   the waters stood abóve the mountains.
⁷ At your rebúke they fled;
   at the sound of your thunder they fléd in terror.
⁸ They rose up to the mountains, ran down tó the valleys,
   to the place which you appóinted for them.
⁹ **You set a boundary which they cánnot pass,**
   so that they might not again cóver the earth.
¹⁰ You make springs gush forth ín the valleys;
    they flow betwéen the hills;
¹¹ **they give drink to every beast óf the field;**
    the wild asses quénch their thirst.
¹² Above the springs the birds of the air háve their nests;
    they sing amóng the branches.
¹³ **From your lofty dwelling you wáter the mountains;**
    the earth is satisfied with the fruit óf your work.   R

¹⁴ You cause the grass to grów for cattle,
    and plants for people to use,
    to bring forth food fróm the earth,
¹⁵ **wine to gladden the húman heart,**
    oil to make the face shine,
    and bread to strengthen the húman heart.
¹⁶ The trees of the Lord are watered abúndantly,
    the cedars of Lebanon thát God planted.
¹⁷ **In them the birds búild their nests;**
    the stork has its home in thé fir trees.
¹⁸ The high mountains are fór wild goats;
    the rocks are a refuge fór the rodents.
¹⁹ **You have made the moon to márk the seasons;**
    the sun knows its tíme for setting.

20 You make darkness, and ít is night,
    when all the animals of the fórest creep forth.
21 **The young lions roar fór their prey,**
    seeking their fóod from God.
22 When the sun rises, théy withdraw
    and lie down ín their dens.
23 **People go out tó their work,**
    to their labor untíl the evening.   **R**

24 O Lord, how vast áre your works!
    In wisdom you have made them all;
    the earth is full óf your creatures.
25 There is the sea, great and wide,
    innumerable créatures are there,
    living things both gréat and small.
26 Sea monsters live there,
    Leviathan, which you formed, pláys in it.
27 **These all look to you,**
    to give them their food ín due season.
28 When you give it to them, they gáther it.
    when you open your hand, they are filled wíth good things.
29 When you hide your face, they áre dismayed;
    when you take away their breath, they die
    and return tó their dust.
30 When you send forth your spirit, they áre created;
    and you renew the face óf the earth.
31 May the glory of the Lord endúre forever,
    may the Lord rejoice ín these works.
32 **The Lord looks on the earth ánd it trembles,**
    and touches the mountains ánd they smoke!
33 I will sing to the Lord as long ás I live!
    I will sing praise to my God contínually.
34 May my meditation be pleasing to the Lord in whom Í rejoice.
35 **Let sinners be consumed from the earth,**
    and let the wicked bé no more!
    Bless the Lord, Ó my soul!
    Praise thé Lord!   **R**

Psalm 105

R

1 O give thanks to the Lord, call ón God's name,
    make known God's deeds amóng the peoples!
2 **Sing to the Lórd, sing praises!**
    Tell of all God's wónderful works!
3 Glory in God's hóly name;
    let the hearts of those who seek the Lórd rejoice!

⁴ **Seek the Lord, the strength óf the Lord;**
  seek the Lord's presence contínually!
⁵ Remember the wonderful works Gód has done,
  the miracles and judgments Gód has uttered,
⁶ **O offspring of Abraham, Gód's servant,**
  children of Jacob, God's chósen ones.   R

⁷ The Lord ís our God,
  whose judgments are in áll the earth.
⁸ **The Lord is mindful of the everlasting cóvenant.**
  of the word commanded for a thousand génerations,
⁹ the covenant made with Ábraham,
  the promise swórn to Isaac,
¹⁰ and confirmed to Jacob ás a statute,
  to Israel as an everlasting cóvenant, saying,
¹¹ **"To you I will give the lánd of Canaan**
  as your portion for an inhéritance."   R

¹² When they were féw in number,
  of little account, and stróngers in it,
¹³ wandering from nátion to nation,
  from one kingdom to anóther people,
¹⁴ God allowed no one tó oppress them,
  and rebuked kings on théir account,
¹⁵ saying, "Do not touch my anóinted ones;
  do my próphets no harm."
¹⁶ **When God summoned famine agáinst the land,**
  and destroyed every sóurce of food,
¹⁷ **God had sent a man ahéad of them,**
  Joseph, who was sold ás a slave.
¹⁸ His feet were húrt with fetters,
  his neck was put in a cóllar of iron,
¹⁹ until what he had said cáme to pass,
  the word of the Lord kept tésting him.
²⁰ **The king sent ánd released him,**
  the ruler of the peoples sét him free;
²¹ **he made him head óf his house,**
  and ruler of all hís possessions,
²² **to instruct his officials át his pleasure,**
  and to teach his élders wisdom.
²³ Then Israel cáme to Egypt;
  Jacob lived as an alien in the lánd of Ham.
²⁴ **And the Lord made them véry fruitful,**
  made them stronger thán their foes,
²⁵ whose hearts God changed to háte this people,
  to deal craftily with God's servants.   R

26 The Lord sent the sérvant Moses,
   and Aaron whom Gód had chosen.
27 **They performed God's signs ámong them,**
   and miracles in the lánd of Ham.
28 The Lord sent darkness, and made thé land dark;
   they rebelled agáinst God's words.
29 **The Lord turned their waters ínto blood,**
   and caused their físh to die.
30 Their land swármed with frogs,
   even in the chambers óf their kings.
31 **The Lord spoke, and there came swárms of flies**
   and gnats throughóut their country.
32 The Lord gave them háil for rain,
   and lightning that flashed thróugh their land,
33 struck their vines ánd fig trees,
   and shattered the trees óf their country.
34 **The Lord spoke, and the lócusts came,**
   and young locusts wíthout number;
35 they devoured all the vegetation ín their land,
   and ate up the fruit óf their ground.
36 **The Lord struck down all the first-born ín their land,**
   the first issue of áll their strength.   R

37 Then the Lord brought Israel out with sílver and gold,
   and there was no one among the tríbes who stumbled.
38 **Egypt was glad when théy departed,**
   for dread of them had fallen úpon it.
39 The Lord spread a cloud for cóvering,
   and fire to give líght by night.
40 **They asked, and Gód brought quails,**
   and gave them food from heaven ín abundance.
41 The Lord opened the rock, and wáter gushed out;
   it flowed through the desert líke a river.
42 **For the Lord remembered the hóly promise,**
   and Abraham, Gód's servant.
43 So the Lord brought Israel óut with joy,
   God's chosen ónes with singing.
44 **The Lord gave them the lands óf the nations,**
   and they took possession of the wealth óf the peoples,
45 **that they might keep God's statutes,**
   and obsérve God's laws.
   Praise thé Lord!   R

Psalm 106

R

¹ Praise thé Lord!
O give thanks to the Lord who is good;
whose steadfast love endúres forever!
² Who can utter the mighty doings óf the Lord,
or show forth áll God's praise?
³ **Blessed are those who obsérve justice,**
who do righteousness át all times!
⁴ Remember me, O Lord, when you show favor tó your people;
help me when you delíver them,
⁵ **that I may see the prosperity of your chósen ones,**
that I may rejoice in the gladness of your nation,
that I may glory with your héritage.   R

⁶ Both we and our ancéstors have sinned;
we have committed iniquity, we have done wíckedly.
⁷ **Our ancestors, when they wére in Egypt,**
did not consider your wónderful works;
they did not remember the abundance of your stéadfast love,
but rebelled against the Most High at thé Red Sea.
⁸ **For the sake of the holy name, Gód saved them**
to make known the mighty pówer of God.
⁹ God rebuked the Red Sea, and it becáme dry;
and led them through the deep as thróugh a desert.
¹⁰ **So God saved them from the hand óf the foe,**
and delivered them from the hand of the énemy.
¹¹ The waters covered their ádversaries;
not one of thém was left.
¹² **Then they belíeved God's words;**
they sáng God's praise.   R

¹³ But they soon forgót God's works;
they did not wait fór God's counsel.
¹⁴ **But they had a craving in the wílderness,**
and put God to the test ín the desert,
¹⁵ **who gave them whát they asked,**
but sent a wasting diséase among them.
¹⁶ They were jealous of Moses ín the camp,
and of Aaron, the holy one óf the Lord.
¹⁷ **The earth opened and swállowed up Dathan,**
and covered the faction of Ábiram.
¹⁸ Fire also broke out in their cómpany;
the flame burned úp the wicked.
¹⁹ **They made a cálf at Horeb**
and worshiped a mólten image.

133

20 They exchanged the glóry of God
for the image of an ox thát eats grass.
21 **They forgot Gód, their Savior,**
who had done great thíngs in Egypt,
22 **wondrous works in the lánd of Ham,**
and awesome deeds by thé Red Sea.
23 Therefore the Lord intended to destroy them
had not Moses, the chósen one,
stood in the breach,
to turn away God's desire tó destroy.
24 **Then they despised the pléasant land,**
having no faith ín God's promise.
25 They grumbled ín their tents,
and did not obey the voice óf the Lord.
26 **Therefore, with uplifted hánd God swore**
to make them fall in the wílderness,
27 **and disperse their descendants amóng the nations,**
scattering them óver the lands.   R

28 Then they attached themselves to the Báal of Peor,
and ate sacrifices offered tó the dead;
29 they provoked the Lord to anger wíth their deeds,
and a plague broke out ámong them.
30 **Then Phineas stood up and ínterceded**
and the plágue was stopped.
31 **And that has been counted to him as ríghteousness**
from generation to generation foréver.
32 They angered God at the waters of Méribah,
and it went badly for Moses on théir account;
33 for they made his spírit bitter,
and he spoke words thát were rash.
34 **They did not destróy the peoples,**
as the Lord commánded them,
35 **but they mingled wíth the nations**
and learned to do ás they did.
36 They served their idols,
which became a snáre to them.
37 **They sacrificed their sons**
and their dáughters to demons;
38 they poured out ínnocent blood,
the blood of their sóns and daughters,
whom they sacrificed to the ídols of Canaan;
and the land was pollúted with blood.
39 **Thus they became unclean bý their deeds,**
and acted like whores ín their doings.   R

40 The anger of the Lord was kindled agáinst this people;
God abhorred this héritage,
41 and gave them into the hand óf the nations,
so that those who hated them ruled óver them.
42 **Their enemies oppréssed them,**
and they were brought into subjection únder their power.
43 Many times God delívered them,
but they were rebellious in their purposes,
and were brought low through their iníquity.
44 **Nevertheless, God heard their cry**
and regarded théir distress.
45 **God remembered the covenant for their sake,**
and showed compassion in boundless stéadfast love.
46 God caused them tó be pitied
by all who héld them captive.
47 **Save us, O Lord our God,**
and gather us from amóng the nations,
that we may give thanks to your holy name
and glory ín your praise.
48 Blessed be the Lord, the God of Ísrael,
from everlasting to éverlasting!
And let all the people sáy "Amen!"
Praise thé Lord!   **R**

Psalm 107

R

1 O give thanks to the Lord, whó is good,
whose steadfast love endúres forever!
2 **Let the redeemed of the Lórd say so,**
whom the Lord has redéemed from trouble
3 **and gathered in fróm the lands,**
from the east and from the west,
from the north and fróm the south.
4 Some wandered in the désert wastes,
finding no way to a city in whích to dwell;
5 **hungry and thirsty,**
their soul fainted withín them.
6 Then in their trouble, they cried to the Lord,
who delivered them from théir distress,
7 **and led them by á straight way,**
till they reached a city in whích to dwell.
8 Let them thank the Lord for stéadfast love,
for wonderful works to húmankind.
9 **For the Lord satisfies those whó are thirsty,**
and fills the hungry wíth good things.   **R**

10 Some sat in darkness ánd in gloom,
   prisoners in misery ánd in irons,
11 for they had rebelled against the wórds of God,
   and spurned the counsel of thé Most High.
12 **Their hearts were bowed down wíth hard labor;**
   they fell down, with no óne to help.
13 Then they cried to the Lord ín their trouble,
   who saved them from théir distress,
14 who brought them out of dárkness and gloom,
   and broke their bónds asunder.
15 **Let them thank the Lord for stéadfast love,**
   for wonderful works to húmankind.
16 **For God shatters the dóors of bronze,**
   and cuts in two the bárs of iron.   R

17 Some were fools through their sínful ways,
   and because of their iniquities endúred affliction;
18 they loathed any kínd of food,
   and they drew near to the gátes of death.
19 **Then they cried to the Lord ín their trouble,**
   who saved them from théir distress,
20 **who sent out God's wórd and healed them,**
   and delivered them fróm destruction.
21 Let them thank the Lord for stéadfast love,
   for wonderful works to húmankind.
22 **And let them offer sacrifices óf thanksgiving,**
   and tell of God's deeds with sóngs of joy.   R

23 Some went down to the séa in ships,
   doing business on the míghty waters;
24 they saw the deeds óf the Lord,
   God's wonderous works ín the deep.
25 **For God commanded and raised the stórmy wind,**
   which lifted up the waves óf the sea.
26 They mounted up to heaven, they went down tó the depths;
   their courage melted away in their calámity;
27 they reeled and stággered like drunkards,
   and were at théir wits' end.
28 **Then they cried to the Lord ín their trouble,**
   and God brought them out of théir distress,
29 **made the stórm be still,**
   and the waves of the séa were hushed.
30 Then they were glad because théy had quiet,
   and God brought them to their desíred haven.
31 **Let them thank the Lord for stéadfast love,**
   for wonderful works to húmankind.

32 Let them extol God in the congregation óf the people,
     and praise God in the assembly óf the elders.   R
33 The Lord turns rivers ínto a desert,
     springs of water into thírsty ground,
34 **a fruitful land into a sálty waste,**
     because of the wickedness of its inhábitants.
35 The Lord turns a desert into póols of water,
     a parched land into spríngs of water.
36 **The Lord lets the húngry dwell there,**
     and they establish a city in whích to live;
37 they sow fields, and plánt vineyards,
     and get a frúitful yield.
38 **They multiply greatly by the blessing óf the Lord,**
     who does not let their cáttle decrease.
39 When they are diminished ánd brought low
     through oppression, tróuble, and sorrow,
40 the Lord pours contempt úpon princes
     and makes them wander in tráckless wastes;
41 **But the Lord raises up the needy out of mísery,**
     and makes their fámilies like flocks.
42 The upright see it ánd are glad;
     and all wickedness stóps its mouth.
43 **Whoever is wise, give heed tó these things,**
     and consider the steadfast love óf the Lord.   R

Psalm 108

R

1 My heart is steadfast, O God, my héart is steadfast;
     I will sing and make melody.
     Awáke, my soul!
2 **Awake, O hárp and lyre!**
     I will awáke the dawn.
3 I will give thanks to you, O Lord, amóng the peoples,
     I will sing praises to you amóng the nations.
4 **For your steadfast love is higher thán the heavens,**
     your faithfulness reaches tó the clouds.
5 Be exalted, O God, abóve the heavens,
     let your glory be over áll the earth.
6 **Save with your right hand, and ánswer me,**
     so that those whom you love may bé rescued.   R

7   God has spoken in hóliness:
     "With rejoicing I will divide up Shechem,
     and portion out the pláin of Succoth.

8   **Gilead is mine; Manássah is mine;**
     Ephraim is my helmet;
     Judah ís my scepter.

9   Moab is my wáshbasin;
     on Edom I hurl my shoe;
     over Philistia I shóut in triumph."

10   **Who will bring me to the fórtified city?**
     Who will lead mé to Edom?

11   Have you not rejected ús, O God?
     You do not go out, O God, wíth our armies.

12   **O grant us help agáinst the foe,**
     for human hélp is worthless.

13   With God we shall áct with strength;
     it is God who will tread dówn our foes.   **R**

Psalm 109

R

1   Do not be silent, O God óf my praise,

2   for wicked and deceitful mouths are opened against me,
     speaking against me with lýing tongues.

3   **They surround me with wórds of hate,**
     and attack me wíthout cause.

4   In return for my love théy accuse me,
     even while I make práyer for them.

5   **So they reward me évil for good,**
     and hatred fór my love.   R

6   Appoint a wicked one ágainst them;
     let an accuser stand ón their right.

7   **When they are tried, let them cóme forth wicked;**
     let their prayer becóme sin.

8   May their dáys be few;
     may another seize théir position.

9   **May their chíldren be orphans,**
     and their wíves widows.

10   May their children wander abóut and beg;
     may they search ónly ruins.

11   **May the creditor seize all thát they have;**
     may strangers plunder the fruits óf their toil.

12   May there be none to dó them kindness,
     nor any to pity their órphaned children.

¹³ **May their posterity bé cut off;**
may their name be blotted out in the second géneration.

¹⁴ May their ancestors' iniquity be remembered befóre the Lord,
and do not let the sin of their mothers be blótted out.

¹⁵ **Let them be continually befóre the Lord,**
and may their memory be cut off fróm the earth.

¹⁶ For they did not remember to shów kindness,
but pursued the poor and needy
and the brokenhearted tó their death.

¹⁷ **They loved to curse; let curses cóme on them.**
They did not like the blessing; may it be fár from them.

¹⁸ They clothed themselves with cursing ás their coat,
may it soak into their bodies like water,
like oil intó their bones.

¹⁹ **May it be like a garment that they wrap aróund them,**
like a belt that they wear évery day. **R**

²⁰ May this be the reward of my accusers fróm the Lord,
of those who speak evil agáinst my life.

²¹ **But you, O Lord my Lord,**
act on my behalf for yóur name's sake;
because your steadfast love is good, delíver me.

²² For I am póor and needy,
and my heart is pierced wíthin me.

²³ **I am gone, like a shádow at evening;**
I am shaken off líke a locust.

²⁴ My knees are wéak through fasting;
my body has becóme gaunt.

²⁵ **I am an object of scorn to mý accusers;**
when they see me, they sháke their heads.

²⁶ Help me, O Lórd my God!
Save me according to your stéadfast love.

²⁷ **Let them know that this ís your hand;**
you, O Lórd, have done it.

²⁸ Let them curse, but yóu will bless.
Let my assailants be put to shame; may your sérvant be glad.

²⁹ **May my accusers be clothed wíth dishonor;**
may they be wrapped in their own shame as ín a robe.

³⁰ With my mouth I will give great thanks tó the Lord;
I will praise God in the midst óf a throng.

³¹ **For God stands at the right hand óf the needy,**
to save them from those who condemn thém to death. **R**

Psalm 110

R

1 The Lord says to my master:
  "Sit at mý right hand,
  until I make your enemies your fóotstool."
2 The Lord sends out from Zion
  your míghty scepter:
  "Rule in the midst óf your foes.
3 **Your people will offer themselves willingly**
  on the day you lead your host
  in hóly splendor.
  From the womb of the morning
  will come the dew óf your youth."
4 The Lord has sworn and wíll not change,
  "You are a priest forever after the order of Melchízedek."
5 The Lord is at yóur right hand,
  and will destroy kings on the day óf God's wrath,
6 will judge the nations,
  filling thém with corpses,
  and will destroy the leaders
  across thé wide earth.
7 **My master will drink from the brook bý the path;**
  and will aríse as leader.   R

Psalm 111

R

1 Praise the Lord!
  I will give thanks to the Lord with mý whole heart,
  in the company of the upright, in the cóngregation.
2 Great are the works óf the Lord,
  studied by all who delíght in them.
3 **Full of honor and majesty are the works óf the Lord**
  whose righteousness endúres forever,
4 who has given us a memory of these wónderful works;
  the Lord is gracious and mérciful.
5 **The Lord provides food for those whó are faithful**
  and is ever mindful of the cóvenant.   R

6 The Lord has shown God's people the power óf these works;
  by giving them the heritage óf the nations.
7 **The works of the Lord's hands are fáithful and just;**
  the precepts of the Lord are trústworthy;
8 they are established foréver and ever,
  to be performed with faithfulness and úprightness.

⁹ The Lord sent redemption to this people;
and has commanded the cóvenant forever.
Holy and wondrous ís God's name!
¹⁰ **The fear of the Lord is the beginning of wisdom;**
all those who practice it have a good únderstanding,
The praise of the Lord endúres forever.   R

Psalm 112

R

¹ Praise the Lord!
Blessed are those who féar the Lord,
who greatly delight in Gód's commandments!
² **Their descendants will be mighty ín the land;**
the generation of the upright wíll be blessed.
³ Wealth and riches are ín their houses,
and their righteousness endúres forever.
⁴ **They rise in darkness as a light for thé upright;**
they are gracious, mercifúl and righteous.
⁵ It is well with those who are génerous and lend,
who conduct their affáirs with justice.
⁶ **For the righteous shall néver be moved;**
they will be remémbered forever.
⁷ They are not afraid of évil news;
their hearts are firm, secure ín the Lord.
⁸ **When they see their ádversaries,**
their hearts are steady, they will not bé afraid.
⁹ They have distributed freely, they have given tó the poor;
their righteousness endures forever;
their horn is exálted in honor.
¹⁰ **The wicked see it and are angry;**
they gnash their teeth and mélt away;
the desire of the wicked cómes to nothing.   R

Psalm 113

R

¹ Praise the Lord!
Praise, O servants óf the Lord,
praise the name óf the Lord!
² Blessed be the name óf the Lord
from this time forth and for évermore!
³ **From the rising of the sun tó its setting**
the name of the Lord is tó be praised!
⁴ The Lord is high abóve all nations,
God's glory abóve the heavens!

⁵ **Who is like the Lord our God,**
   who is séated on high,
⁶ **who looks far down**
   upon the heavens ánd the earth?
⁷ God raises the poor fróm the dust,
   and lifts the needy from thé ash heap,
⁸ to make them sít with nobles,
   with the nobles óf God's people.
⁹ **God gives the barren woman a home,**
   making her the joyous móther of children.
   Praise thé Lord!   R

Psalm 114

R

¹ When Israel went fórth from Egypt,
   the house of Jacob from a people óf strange language,
² **Judah became God's sánctuary,**
   Israel Gód's dominion.
³ The sea looked and fled,
   Jórdan turned back.
⁴ **The mountains skipped like rams,**
   the hílls like lambs.
⁵ O sea, why dó you flee?
   O Jordan, why do yóu turn back?
⁶ **O mountains, why do you skíp like rams?**
   O hílls, like lambs?
⁷ Tremble, O earth, at the presence óf the Lord,
   at the presence of the Gód of Jacob,
⁸ **who turns the rock into a póol of water,**
   the flint into a spríng of water.   R

Psalm 115

R

¹ Not to us, O Lord,
   not to us, but to your náme give glory,
   for the sake of your steadfast love and fáithfulness!
² Why should the nations say,
   "Where ís their God?"
³ **Our God is in the heavens;**
   whatever God pléases, God does.
⁴ Their idols are silver and gold,
   the work of húman hands.
⁵ **They have mouths, but do not speak;**
   eyes, but dó not see.

6 They have ears, but do not hear;
   noses, but dó not smell.
7 **They have hands, but do not feel;**
   feet, but do not walk;
   throats, but máke no sound.
8 Those who make idols áre like them;
   so are all who trúst in them.
9 O, Israel, trust ín the Lord!
   The Lord is their help ánd their shield.
10 O house of Aaron, trust ín the Lord!
   The Lord is their help ánd their shield.
11 You who fear the Lord, trust ín the Lord!
   The Lord is their help ánd their shield.   **R**

12 The Lord has been mindful of us and will bless us,
   will bless the house of Israel,
   will bless the hóuse of Aaron,
13 and will bless those who fear the Lord,
   both gréat and small.
14 **May the Lord give you increase,**
   both you ánd your children.
15 **May you be blessed by the Lord,**
   who made héaven and earth.
16 The heavens are the Lórd's heavens,
   but the earth God has gíven to mortals.
17 **The dead do not práise the Lord,**
   nor do any that go down ínto silence.
18 But we will bless the Lord
   now ánd forever.
   Praise thé Lord!   **R**

Psalm 116

R

1 I love the Lord, who has heard
   my voice and my súpplications,
2 and has listened to me
   whenéver I called.
3 **The snares of death encompassed me;**
   the pangs of Sheol laid hóld on me;
   I suffered distréss and anguish.
4 Then I called on the name óf the Lord:
   "O Lord, I pray, sáve my life!"
5 Gracious is the Lórd, and righteous;
   our God is mérciful.

143

6   **The Lord presérves the simple;**
     when I was brought low, the Lórd saved me.
7   Return, O my soul, tó your rest;
     for the Lord has dealt bountifully wíth you.
8   For you have delivered my lífe from death,
     my eyes from tears,
     my féet from stumbling;
9   **I walk befóre the Lord**
     in the land óf the living.
10   I kept my faith, even whén I said,
     "I am greatly afflícted."
11   **I said in my cónsternation,**
     "All humans are á vain hope."   **R**

12   What shall I return tó the Lord
     for all God's gífts to me?
13   **I will lift up the cup óf salvation**
     and call on the name óf the Lord,
14   I will pay my vows tó the Lord
     in the presence of áll God's people.
15   **Precious in the sight óf the Lord**
     is the death óf the faithful.
16   O Lord, I am your servant;
     I am your servant, the child of yóur handmaid.
     You have lóosed my bonds.
17   **I will offer to you the sacrifice óf thanksgiving**
     and call on the name óf the Lord.
18   I will pay my vows tó the Lord,
     in the presence of áll God's people,
19   **in the courts of the house of the Lord,**
     in your midst, O Jerúsalem.
     Praise thé Lord!   **R**

Psalm 117

R

1   Praise the Lórd, all nations!
     Extol the Lórd, all peoples!
2   Great is the Lord's steadfast lóve toward us!
     The faithfulness of the Lord endures forever!
     Praise thé Lord!   **R**

Psalm 118

R

¹ O give thanks to the Lord, whó is good;
    whose steadfast love endúres forever!
² **Let Ísrael say,**
    "God's steadfast love endúres forever."
³ Let the house of Áaron say,
    "God's steadfast love endúres forever."
⁴ **Let those who fear thé Lord say,**
    "God's steadfast love endúres forever."
⁵ Out of my distress I called ón the Lord;
    the Lord answered me and set me in á broad place.
⁶ With the Lord on my side I dó not fear.
    What can mortals dó to me?
⁷ The Lord is on my side tó help me;
    I shall look in triumph on thóse who hate me.
⁸ It is better to take refuge ín the Lord
    than to put confidénce in mortals.
⁹ **It is better to take refuge ín the Lord**
    than to put confidénce in nobles.   **R**

¹⁰ All nations surróunded me;
    in the name of the Lord I cút them off!
¹¹ **They surrounded me, surrounded me on évery side;**
    in the name of the Lord I cút them off!
¹² They surrounded me like bees,
    they blazed like a fíre of thorns;
    in the name of the Lord I cút them off!
¹³ **I was pushed hard, so that Í was falling,**
    but the Lórd helped me.
¹⁴ The Lord is my strength ánd my power;
    the Lord has become mý salvation.
¹⁵ **There are joyous songs of victory**
    in the tents óf the righteous:
    "The right hand of the Lord does valiantly,
¹⁶   the right hand of the Lord is exalted,
    the right hand of the Lord does váliantly!"
¹⁷ I shall not die, but Í shall live,
    and recount the deeds óf the Lord.
¹⁸ **The Lord disciplined mé severely,**
    but did not give me óver to death.
¹⁹ Open to me the gates of ríghteousness,
    that I may enter through them
    and give thanks tó the Lord.
²⁰ **This is the gate óf the Lord;**
    the righteous shall énter through it.

21 I thank you that you have ánswered me
  and have become mý salvation.
22 **The stone which the buílders rejected**
  has become the córnerstone.
23 This is the Lord's doing;
  it is marvelous ín our eyes.
24 **This is the day which the Lord has made;**
  let us rejoice and be glád in it.   R

25 Save us, we beseech yóu, O Lord!
  O Lord, we beseech you, give ús success!
26 Blessed is the one who comes in the name óf the Lord!
  We bless you from the house óf the Lord.
27 The Lord is God,
  who has gíven us light.
  Lead the festal procession with branches,
  up to the horns óf the altar!
28 You are my God, and I will give thánks to you;
  you are my God, I wíll extol you.
29 **O give thanks to the Lord, whó is good;**
  for God's steadfast love endúres forever!   R

Psalm 119

R

1 Blessed are those whose wáy is blameless,
  who walk in the law óf the Lord!
2 **Blessed are those who keep God's téstimonies,**
  who seek God with théir whole heart,
3 who also dó no wrong,
  but walk ín God's ways!
4 **You have commanded your precepts**
  to be kept díligently.
5 O that my ways may be steadfast
  in kéeping your statutes!
6 **Then I shall not be put to shame,**
  having my eyes fixed on all yóur
  commandments.
7 I will praise you with an upright heart,
  when I learn your righteous órdinances.
8 **I will observe your statutes;**
  Do not ever abándon me!   R

⁹ How can the young keep théir way pure?
   By guarding it according tó your word.
¹⁰ **With my whole heart Í seek you;**
   do not let me stray from yóur commandments!
¹¹ I treasure your word ín my heart,
   that I may not sin ágainst you.
¹² **Blessed are you, O Lord;**
   teach mé your statutes;
¹³ With my lips I declare
   all the ordinances óf your mouth.
¹⁴ **I delight in the way of your testimonies**
   as much as ín all riches.
¹⁵ I will meditate on your precepts,
   and fix my eyes ón your ways.
¹⁶ **I will delight ín your statutes;**
   I will not forgét your word.   R

¹⁷ Deal bountifully with your servant,
   that I may live and obsérve your word.
¹⁸ **Open my eyes, that I may behold**
   wondrous things out óf your law.
¹⁹ I live as an alien in the land;
   do not hide your commándments from me.
²⁰ **My soul is consumed with longing**
   for your ordinances át all times.
²¹ You rebuke the insolent, the accursed ones,
   who wander from yóur commandments;
²² **take away from me their scorn and contempt,**
   for I have kept your téstimonies.
²³ Even though princes sit plotting against me,
   your servant will meditate ón your statutes.
²⁴ **Your testimonies are my delight,**
   they are my cóunselors.   R

²⁵ My life clings to the dust;
   revive me according tó your word.
²⁶ **When I spoke of my ways, you answered me;**
   teach mé your statutes.
²⁷ Make me understand the way of your precepts,
   and I will meditate on your wóndrous works.
²⁸ My life melts away for sorrow;
   strengthen me according tó your word.
²⁹ **Put false ways far from me,**
   and graciously teach mé your law.
³⁰ I have chosen the way of faithfulness;
   I set your ordinances befóre me.

31 I cling to your testimonies, O Lord;
    do not let me be pút to shame.
32 **I run the course with your commandments,**
    for you enlarge my únderstanding.   **R**

33 Teach me, O Lord, the way of your statutes;
    and I will keep it tó the end.
34 **Give me understanding, that I may keep your law**
    and observe it with mý whole heart.
35 Lead me in the path of your commandments,
    for I delíght in it.
36 **Turn my heart to your testimonies,**
    and nót to gain!
37 Turn my eyes from looking at vanities;
    and give me life ín your ways.
38 **Confirm to your servant your promise,**
    which is for thóse who fear you.
39 Turn away the scorn which I dread;
    for your ordinances áre good.
40 **See, I long for your precepts;**
    in your righteousness gíve me life!
41 Let your steadfast love come to me, O Lord,
    your salvation according tó your promise;
42 **then shall I have an answer for those who taunt me,**
    for I trust ín your word.
43 Do not take the word of truth utterly out of my mouth,
    for my hope is in your órdinances.
44 **I will keep your law continually,**
    forevér and ever;
45 and I shall walk at liberty,
    for I have sóught your precepts.
46 **I will also speak of your testimonies before rulers,**
    and shall not be pút to shame;
47 for I find my delight in your commandments,
    whích I love.
48 **I revere your commandments, which I love,**
    and I will meditate ón your statutes.   **R**

49 Remember your word to your servant,
    in which you have máde me hope.
50 **This is my comfort in my distress,**
    that your promise gíves me life.
51 The arrogant utterly deríde me,
    but I do not turn away fróm your law.

52   When I remember your judgments fróm of old,
     I take cómfort, O Lord.
53   Hot indignation seizes me because of the wicked,
     those who forsáke your law.
54   **Your statutes have been my songs**
     wherever I máke my home.
55   I remember your name in the night, O Lord,
     and kéep your law.
56   **This blessing has fallen to me,**
     for I have képt your precepts.   **R**

57   The Lord is my portion;
     I promise to kéep your words.
58   **I implore your favor with all my heart;**
     be gracious to me according tó your promise.
59   When I think of your ways,
     I turn my feet to your téstimonies;
60   **I hurry and do not delay**
     to keep yóur commandments.
61   Though the cords of the wicked entangle me,
     I do not forgét your law.
62   **At midnight I rise to praise you,**
     because of your righteous órdinances.
63   I am a companion of all who fear you,
     of those who kéep your precepts.
64   **O Lord, the earth is full of your steadfast love;**
     teach mé your statutes!   **R**

65   You have dealt well with your servant,
     O Lord, according tó your word.
66   **Teach me good judgment and knowledge,**
     for I believe in yóur commandments.
67   Before I was humbled I went astray,
     but now I kéep your word.
68   **You are good and do good;**
     teach mé your statutes.
69   The arrogant smear me with lies,
     but with my whole heart I kéep your precepts.
70   **Their hearts are gorged with fat,**
     but I delight ín your law.
71   It is good for me that I was humbled,
     so that I might léarn your statutes.
72   **The law of your mouth is better to me**
     than thousands of gold and sílver pieces.   **R**

73   Your hands have made and fáshioned me;
       give me understanding that I may learn yóur commandments.
74   **Those who fear you shall see me ánd rejoice,**
       because I have hoped ín your word.
75   I know, O Lord, that your júdgments are right,
       and that in faithfulness you have húmbled me.
76   **Let your steadfast love becóme my comfort**
       according to your promise tó your servant.
77   Let your mercy come to me, that Í may live;
       for your law is mý delight.
78   **Let the arrogant be put to shame,**
       because they have misled mé with lies;
       as for me, I will meditate ón your precepts.
79   Let those who fear you túrn to me,
       that they may know your téstimonies.
80   **May my heart be blameless ín your statutes,**
       that I may not be pút to shame.   R

81   My life longs for yóur salvation;
       I hope ín your word.
82   **My eyes fail with watching fór your promise;**
       I ask, "When will you cómfort me?"
83   For I have become like a wineskin fílled with mist,
       yet I have not forgótten your statutes.
84   **How long must your sérvant endure?**
       When will you judge those who pérsecute me?
85   The arrogant have dug pitfalls for me;
       they móck your law.
86   **All your commandments are enduring;**
       I am persecuted without cáuse; help me!
87   They have almost made an end of mé on earth;
       but I have not forsáken your precepts.
88   **With your steadfast love spáre my life,**
       that I may keep the testimonies óf your mouth.   R

89   The Lord lives forever;
       your word is firmly fixed ín the heavens.
90   **Your faithfulness endures to all generations;**
       you have established the earth, and ít stands fast.
91   By your judgments they stand today,
       for all things áre your servants.
92   **If your law had not been my delight,**
       I would have perished ín my misery.
93   I will never forget your precepts,
       for by them you have gíven me life.

94 I am yours; save me,
        for I have sóught your precepts.
95 The wicked lie in wait to destroy me,
        but I consider your téstimonies.
96 I have seen an end to all accomplishment,
        but your commándment is endless.   R

97 Oh, how I love your law!
        It is my meditation áll day long.
98 Your commandment makes me wiser than my enemies,
        for it is álways with me.
99 I have more understanding than all my teachers,
        for your testimonies are my méditation.
100 I understand more than the aged,
        for I kéep your precepts.
101 I hold back my feet from every evil way,
        in order to kéep your word.
102 I do not turn away from your ordinances,
        for you have táught me.
103 How sweet are your words to my taste,
        sweeter than honey tó my mouth!
104 Through your precepts I get understanding;
        therefore I hate every fálse way.   R

105 Your word is a lamp to my feet
        and a light tó my path.
106 I have sworn an oath and confirmed it,
        to observe your righteous órdinances.
107 I am severely afflicted;
        give me life, O Lord, according tó your word.
108 Accept my offerings of praise, O Lord,
        and teach me your órdinances.
109 I hold my life in my hand continually,
        but I do not forgét your law.
110 The wicked have laid a snare for me,
        but I do not stray fróm your precepts.
111 Your testimonies are my heritage forever;
        they are the joy óf my heart.
112 I prepare my heart to perform your statutes
        forever, tó the end.   R

113 I hate the vulgar ones.
        but I lóve your law.
114 You are my hiding place and my shield;
        I hope ín your word.

115 Get away from me, you evildoers,
   that I may keep the commandments óf my God.
116 **Uphold me according to your promise, that I may live,**
   and do not let me be put to shame ín my hope.
117 Hold me up, that I may be safe
   and have regard for your statutes contínually.
118 **You spurn all who go astray from your statutes;**
   for their cunning ís in vain.
119 All the wicked of the earth you count as waste;
   therefore I love your téstimonies.
120 **My flesh trembles for fear of you,**
   and I am afraid óf your judgments.   R

121 I have done what is just and right;
   do not leave me to mý oppressors.
122 **Guarantee your servant's welfare;**
   do not let the insolent oppréss me.
123 My eyes fail watching for your salvation,
   and for the fulfillment of your ríghteousness.
124 **Deal with your servant according to your steadfast love,**
   and teach mé your statutes.
125 I am your servant; give me understanding
   so that I may know your téstimonies.
126 **It is time for the Lord to act,**
   for your law hás been broken.
127 Truly I love your commandments
   more than gold, more thán fine gold.
128 **Truly I direct my steps by all your precepts;**
   I hate every fálse way.   R

129 Your testimonies are wonderful;
   therefore my sóul keeps them.
130 **The unfolding of your words gives light;**
   it imparts understanding tó the simple.
131 With open mouth I pant,
   because I long for yóur commandments.
132 **Turn to me and be gracious to me,**
   for you are just to those who lóve your name.
133 Keep steady my steps according to your promise,
   and let no iniquity get dominion óver me.
134 **Redeem me from human oppression,**
   that I may kéep your precepts.
135 Make your face shine upon your servant,
   and teach mé your statutes.
136 **My eyes shed streams of tears,**
   because your law ís not kept.   R

137 You are righteous, O Lord,
   and your júdgments are right.
138 **You have appointed your testimonies in righteousness**
   and in all fáithfulness.
139 My zeal consumes me,
   because my foes forgét your words.
140 **Your promise is well tried,**
   and your sérvant loves it.
141 I am small and despised,
   yet I do not forgét your precepts.
142 **Your righteousness is righteous forever,**
   and your law ís trustworthy.
143 Trouble and anguish have come upon me,
   but your commandments are mý delight.
144 **Your testimonies are righteous forever;**
   give me understanding that Í may live.   **R**

145 With my whole heart I cry; answer me, O Lord.
   I will kéep your statutes.
146 **I cry to you; save me**
   that I may observe your téstimonies.
147 I rise before dawn and cry for help;
   I hope ín your words.
148 **My eyes are awake before the watches of the night,**
   that I may meditate ón your promise.
149 In your steadfast love hear my voice;
   O Lord, in your justice presérve my life.
150 **Those lewd ones who pursue me draw near;**
   they are far fróm your law.
151 Yet you are near, O Lord,
   and all your commándments are true.
152 **Long ago I learned from your testimonies**
   that you established thém forever.   **R**

153 Look on my misery and deliver me,
   for I do not forgét your law.
154 **Plead my cause and redeem me;**
   give me life according tó your promise!
155 Salvation is far from the wicked,
   for they do not séek your statutes.
156 **Great is your mercy, O Lord;**
   give me my life according tó your justice.
157 Many are my persecutors and my adversaries,
   yet I do not swerve from your téstimonies.

158   **I look at the faithless with disgust,**
     because they do not keep your prómises.

159   Consider how I lóve your precepts;
     preserve my life according to your stéadfast love.

160   **The first of your wórds is truth;**
     and every one of your righteous judgements
      endúres forever.   **R**

161   Nobles persecute me without cause,
     but my heart stands in awe óf your words.

162   **I rejoice at your word**
     like one who fínds great spoil.

163   I hate and abhor falsehood,
     but I lóve your law.

164   **Seven times a day I praise you**
     for your righteous órdinances.

165   Those who love your law have great peace;
     nothing can máke them stumble.

166   **I hope for your salvátion, O Lord,**
     and I keep yóur commandments.

167   I keep your testimonies;
     I love them excéedingly.

168   **I keep your precepts and testimonies,**
     for all my ways áre before you.   **R**

169   Let my cry come before you, O Lord;
     give me understanding according tó your word.

170   **Let my supplication come before you;**
     deliver me according tó your promise.

171   My lips will póur out praise,
     for you teach mé your statutes.

172   **My tongue will sing of your promise,**
     for all your commándments are right.

173   Let your hand be réady to help me,
     for I have chósen your precepts.

174   **I long for your salvation, O Lord,**
     and your law is mý delight.

175   Let me live, that I may praise you,
     and let your ordinances hélp me.

176   **I have gone astray like a lost sheep; seek oút your servant,**
     for I do not forget yóur commandments.   **R**

Psalm 120

R

¹ I cry to the Lord in my distress
that God may ánswer me:
² **"Deliver me, O Lord,**
from lying lips,
from a decéitful tongue."
³ What more shall be done to you,
you decéitful tongue?
What shall be gíven to you?
⁴ **A warrior's sharp arrows,**
hardened in the glowing coals óf the broom tree!
⁵ Woe is me, that I am an alien in Meshech,
that I must live among the ténts of Kedar.
⁶ **Too long have I had my dwelling**
among those whó hate peace.
⁷ **I am for peace;**
but when I speak,
they áre for war!   **R**

Psalm 121

R

¹ I lift up my eyes tó the hills—
from where does mý help come?
² **My help comes fróm the Lord,**
who made héaven and earth.
³ The Lord will not let your fóot be moved,
the Lord who keeps you wíll not slumber.
⁴ **The One who keeps Ísrael**
will neither slúmber nor sleep.
⁵ The Lord ís your keeper;
the Lord is your shade
on yóur right hand.
⁶ **The sun shall not strike yóu by day,**
nor the móon by night.
⁷ The Lord will keep you fróm all evil,
and will kéep your life.
⁸ **The Lord will keep**
your going out and your cóming in
from this time forth and for évermore.   **R**

Psalm 122

R

¹ I was glad when they said to me,
"Let us go to the house óf the Lord!"
² **Our feet were standing**
within your gates, O Jerúsalem!
³ Jerusalem is built as a city
bound tightly together,
⁴ to which the tríbes go up,
the tribes of the Lord,
to give thanks to the name of the Lord,
as was decreed for Ísrael.
⁵ **Thrones for judgment were sét up there,**
the thrones of the hóuse of David.
⁶ Pray for the peace of Jerusalem:
"May they prósper who love you!
⁷ **Peace be within your walls,**
and security withín your towers!"
⁸ For the sake of my relatives and friends,
I will say, "Peace bé within you!"
⁹ **For the sake of the house of the Lord our God,**
I will séek your good.   R

Psalm 123

R

¹ I lift up my éyes to you,
who are enthroned ín the heavens!
² **As the eyes óf the servants**
look to the hand óf their master,
as the eyes of a maidservant
to the hand of her mistress,
so our eyes look tó the Lord,
until our God has mércy on us.
³ Have mercy on us, O Lord, have mércy on us,
for we have had more than enough óf contempt.
⁴ **Our lives have had their fill of the scorn of those who áre at ease,**
of the contempt óf the proud.   R

Psalm 124

R

¹ If it had not been the Lord who was ón our side—
   let Ísrael now say—
² **if it had not been the Lord who was ón our side,**
   when foes rose up agáinst us,
³ **then they would have swallowed us úp alive,**
   when their anger was kindled agáinst us;
⁴ then the flood would have swept ús away,
   the torrent would have gone óver us;
⁵ **then the raging waters**
   would have gone óver us.
⁶ Blessed be the Lord,
   who has not given us
   as prey tó their teeth!
⁷ **We have escaped as a bird**
   from the snare óf the fowlers;
   the snare is broken,
   and we háve escaped!
⁸ **Our help is in the name óf the Lord**
   who made héaven and earth.   **R**

Psalm 125

R

¹ Those who trust in the Lord are like Mount Zion,
   which cannot be moved, but abídes forever.
² **As the mountains surround Jerúsalem,**
   so the Lord surrounds the people of God,
   from this time forth and for évermore.
³ For the scepter of wickedness shall not rest
   on the land allotted tó the righteous,
   so that the righteous extend
   their hands tó do wrong.
⁴ **Do good, O Lord, to those whó are good,**
   and to those who are upright ín their hearts.
⁵ But the Lord will lead away with evildoers
   those who turn aside to their own cróoked ways!
Peace be upon Ísrael!   **R**

Psalm 126

R

¹ When the Lord restored the fortunes of Zion,
we were like thóse who dream.
² **Then our mouth was filled with laughter,**
and our tongue with shóuts of joy;
then it was said among the nations,
"the Lord has done great thíngs for them."
³ **The Lord has done great thíngs for us,**
and wé are glad.
⁴ Restore our fortunes, O Lord,
like the watercourses ín the Negeb!
⁵ **May those who sow in tears**
reap with shóuts of joy!
⁶ Those who go out weeping,
bearing the séed for sowing,
shall come home with shouts of joy,
carrýing their sheaves.   R

Psalm 127

R

¹ Unless the Lord builds the house,
those who build it lábor in vain.
Unless the Lord guards the city,
the guard keeps wátch in vain.
² It is in vain that you rise up early
and go láte to rest,
eating the bread of distressing work;
for God gives sleep to the beloved óf the Lord.
³ **Children are indeed a heritage from the Lord,**
the fruit of the womb á reward.
⁴ Like arrows in the hand of a warrior
are the children óf one's youth.
⁵ **Happy are those who have**
a quiver fúll of them!
They shall not be put to shame
when they speak with their enemies ín the gate.   R

Psalm 128

R

¹ Blessed is every one who féars the Lord,
who walks ín God's ways.
² **You shall eat the fruit of the labor óf your hands;**
you shall be happy, and it shall go wéll with you.
³ Your wife will be like a fruitful vine
withín your house;
your children will be like olive shoots
aróund your table.
⁴ **Thus shall those be blessed**
who féar the Lord.
⁵ The Lord bless yóu from Zion!
May you see the prosperity of Jerusalem
all the days óf your life.
⁶ **May you see your children's children.**
Peace be upon Ísrael!   R

Psalm 129

R

¹ "Often they attacked me from my youth,"
let Ísrael say,
² **"Often they attacked me from my youth,**
yet they have not prevailed agáinst me.
³ **The plowers plowed on my back;**
they made their fúrrows long."
⁴ The Lord is righteous;
and has cut the cords óf the wicked.
⁵ **May all who hate Zion**
be put to shame ánd turned backward.
⁶ Let them be like the grass on the housetops
that withers before ít grows up,
⁷ with which reapers do not fíll their hands
or binders of shéaves their arms,
⁸ **while those who pass by do not say,**
"The blessing of the Lord be upón you!
We bless you in the name óf the Lord!"   R

Psalm 130

R

¹ Out of the depths I cry to yóu, O Lord!
²   Lord, héar my voice!
Let your ears bé attentive
    to the voice of my súpplications!
³ If you, O Lord, should mark iníquities,
    Lord, whó could stand?
⁴ **But there is forgíveness with you,**
    that you máy be worshiped.
⁵ I wait for the Lord, mý soul waits,
    in the Lord's wórd I hope;
⁶ **my soul waits fór the Lord**
    more than watchers for the morning,
    more than watchers fór the morning.
⁷ O Israel, hope ín the Lord!
    For with the Lord there is steadfast love;
    with the Lord there is gréat redemption.
⁸ **The Lord alone will redeem Ísrael**
    from all iníquities.   **R**

Psalm 131

R

¹ O Lord, my heart is not lífted up,
    my eyes are not ráised too high;
I do not occupy mysélf with things
    too great and too márvelous for me.
² But I have calmed and quieted mý life,
    like a weaned child with its mother;
    I am like á weaned child.
³ **O Israel, hope ín the Lord**
    now ánd forever.   **R**

Psalm 132

R

¹ O Lord, in Dávid's favor,
    remember all the hardships hé endured;
² how he swore tó the Lord
    and vowed to the Mighty Óne of Jacob,
³ **"I will not énter my house**
    or get ínto my bed;

⁴ I will not give sleep tó my eyes
    or slumber tó my eyelids,
⁵ **until I find a place fór the Lord,**
    a dwelling place for the Mighty Óne of Jacob."   **R**

⁶ We heard of it in Ephrathah,
    we found it in the fíelds of Jaar.
⁷ **"Let us go to God's dwelling place;**
    let us worship at Gód's footstool."
⁸ Rise up, O Lord, and go to your résting place,
    you and the ark óf your might.
⁹ **Let your priests be clothed with ríghteousness;**
    let your faithful shóut for joy.
¹⁰ **For your servant Dávid's sake**
    do not turn away the face of your anóinted one.   **R**

¹¹ The Lord swore to David a sure oath
    and from it will nót turn back:
    "One from the fruit of your body
    I will set ón your throne.
¹² If your children keep my covenant
    and my testimonies which I sháll teach them,
    their children also
    shall sit upon your thróne forever."
¹³ **For the Lord has chósen Zion,**
    and has desired it for God's hábitation:
¹⁴ "This is my resting pláce forever;
    here I will dwell, for I háve desired it.
¹⁵ **I will abundantly bless íts provisions;**
    I will satisfy its póor with bread.
¹⁶ Its priests I will clothe wíth salvation,
    and its saints will shóut for joy.
¹⁷ **There will I make a horn to spróut for David;**
    I have prepared a lamp for my anóinted one,
¹⁸ **whose enemies I will clóthe with shame,**
    but upon my anointed a crówn shall shine."   **R**

Psalm 133

R

1   Behold, how good and pléasant it is
     when kindred live together in únity!
2   **It is like precious oil on the head,**
     running dówn the beard,
     the beard of Aaron,
     running down on the collar óf his robes!
3   It is like the dew of Hermon
     which falls on the móuntains of Zion!
   For there the Lord has commanded the blessing:
   Lífe forever!   **R**

Psalm 134

R

1   Come, bless the Lord, all you servants óf the Lord,
     who stand by night in the house óf the Lord!
2   Lift up your hands in the holy place,
     and bléss the Lord!
3   **May the Lord who made heaven and earth**
     bless yóu from Zion.   **R**

Psalm 135

R

1   Praise the Lord!
   Praise the name óf the Lord!
     Give praise, O servants óf the Lord,
2   you that stand in the house óf the Lord,
     in the courts of the house óf our God!
3   **Praise the Lord, for the Lórd is good;**
     sing to the Lord's name, for the Lórd is gracious!
4   For the Lord has chosen Jacob ás God's own,
     Israel as God's ówn possession.
5   **For I know that the Lórd is great,**
     and that our Lord is abóve all gods.
6   Whatever the Lord pleases, thé Lord does,
     in heaven and on earth,
     in the seas ánd all deeps.
7   **It is the Lord who makes the clouds rise**
     at the end óf the earth,
     makes lightnings for the rain
     and brings wind from Gód's storehouse.   **R**

8   It was the Lord who struck the first-bórn of Egypt,
        both human beings and ánimals;
9   **who in your midst, O Egypt,**
        sent sígns and wonders
        against Pharaoh and áll his servants;
10   who struck mány nations
        and slew míghty kings,
11   Sihon, king of the Amorites,
        and Og, kíng of Bashan,
        and all the kingdoms óf Canaan,
12   **and gave their land as a héritage,**
        a heritage to God's people Ísrael.
13   Your name, O Lord, endúres forever,
        your renown, O Lord, throughóut all ages.
14   **For the Lord will vindicate the people of Ísrael**
        and have compassion ón God's servants.   R

15   The idols of the nations are sílver and gold,
        the work of húman hands.
16   **They have mouths, but dó not speak,**
        they have eyes, but dó not see,
17   they have ears, but dó not hear,
        and there is no breath ín their mouths.
18   **Those who make them**
        and áll who trust them
        shall becóme like them.
19   O house of Israel, bléss the Lord!
        O house of Aaron, bléss the Lord!
20   O house of Levi, bléss the Lord!
        You that fear the Lord, bléss the Lord!
21   Blessed be the Lord from Zion,
        who resides in Jerúsalem.
     Praise thé Lord!   R

Psalm 136

R

1   O give thanks to the Lord, whó is good,
        God's steadfast love endúres forever.
2   O give thanks to the Gód of gods,
        God's steadfast love endúres forever.
3   O give thanks to the Lórd of lords,
        God's steadfast love endúres forever.
4   God alone dóes great wonders,
        God's steadfast love endúres forever;

163

5 who by understanding máde the heavens,
   God's steadfast love endúres forever;
6 who spread out the earth upón the waters,
   God's steadfast love endúres forever;
7 who made thé great lights,
   God's steadfast love endúres forever;
8 the sun to rule óver the day,
   God's steadfast love endúres forever;
9 the moon and stars to rule óver the night,
   God's steadfast love endúres forever.   **R**

10 God struck the first-bórn of Egypt,
   God's steadfast love endúres forever;
11 and brought Israel out from amóng them,
   God's steadfast love endúres forever;
12 with a strong hand and an óutstretched arm.
   God's steadfast love endúres forever;
13 God divided thé Red Sea,
   God's steadfast love endúres forever;
14 and made Israel pass through the mídst of it,
   God's steadfast love endúres forever;
15 but overthrew Pharaoh and his host in thé Red Sea,
   God's steadfast love endúres forever.   **R**

16 God led the people of Israel through the wílderness,
   God's steadfast love endúres forever;
17 struck dówn great kings,
   God's steadfast love endúres forever;
18 and killed fámous kings,
   God's steadfast love endúres forever;
19 Sihon, king of the Ámorites,
   God's steadfast love endúres forever;
20 and Og, kíng of Bashan,
   God's steadfast love endúres forever;
21 and gave their land as a héritage,
   God's steadfast love endúres forever;
22 a heritage to God's servant Ísrael,
   God's steadfast love endúres forever;
23 God remembered us in our lów estate,
   God's steadfast love endúres forever;
24 rescued us fróm our foes,
   God's steadfast love endúres forever;
25 and gives good tó all flesh,
   God's steadfast love endúres forever.
26 O give thanks to the Gód of heaven,
   God's steadfast love endúres forever.   **R**

Psalm 137

R

1 By the rivers of Babylon,
    there we sat down and wept,
    when we remémbered Zion.
2 **On the willows there**
    we hung úp our lyres.
3 For there our captors
    required óf us songs,
    and our tormentors, mirth, saying,
    "Sing us one of the sóngs of Zion!"
4 **How shall we sing the Lord's song**
    in a fóreign land?
5 If I forget you, O Jerusalem,
    let my ríght hand wither!
6 **Let my tongue stick to the roof of my mouth,**
    if I do not remémber you,
    if I do not set Jerusalem
    above my híghest joy!
7 O Lord, remember against the Edomites,
    the day of Jerúsalem,
    how they said, "Raze it, raze it!
    Down to íts foundations!"
8 O daughter of Babylon, you dévastator!
    Happy shall they be who repay you
    with what you have dóne to us!
9 **Happy shall they be who take your líttle ones**
    and smash them agáinst a rock!   **R**

Psalm 138

R

1 I give you thanks, O Lord, with mý whole heart;
    before the gods I síng your praise;
2 **I bow down toward your hóly temple**
    and give thanks to your name for your steadfast
    love and fáithulness;
    for you have exalted your name and your word
    above éverything.
3 **On the day I called, you answered me,**
    you stréngthened my life.
4 All the rulers of the earth shall praise yóu, O Lord,
    for they have heard the words óf your mouth.
5 They shall sing of the ways óf the Lord,
    for great is the glory óf the Lord.

⁶ For the Lord is high, but regárds the lowly;
   yet knows the conceited fróm afar.
⁷ Though I walk in the midst of trouble,
   you presérve my life;
   you stretch out your hand against the wrath of my enemies
   and your right hand delívers me.
⁸ O Lord, fulfill your purpose for me;
   O Lord, may your steadfast love endúre forever.
   Do not forsake the work óf your hands.   R

Psalm 139

R

¹ O Lord, you have searched me ánd known me!
² **You know when I sit down and when I rise up;**
   you discern my thoughts fróm afar.
³ You search out my path and my lýing down,
   and are acquainted with áll my ways.
⁴ **Even before a word is on my tóngue, O Lord,**
   you know ít completely.
⁵ You pursue me behind and before,
   and lay your hánd upon me.
⁶ **Such knowledge is too wonderful for me;**
   it is so high, I cannót attain it.   R

⁷ Where shall I go fróm your spirit?
   Or where shall I flee fróm your presence?
⁸ If I ascend to heaven, yóu are there!
   If I make my bed in Sheol, yóu are there!
⁹ **If I take the wings óf the morning**
   and dwell in the deepest parts óf the sea,
¹⁰ **even there your hánd shall lead me,**
   and your right hánd shall hold me.
¹¹ If I say, "Let only darkness cóver me,
   and the light about mé be night,"
¹² **even the darkness is not dárk to you,**
   the night is bright as day;
   for darkness is as líght with you.   R

¹³ For it was you who formed my ínward parts,
   you knit me together in my móther's womb.
¹⁴ I praise you, for I am fearfully and wónderfully made.
   Wonderful áre your works!

You know me very well;
>
> my frame was not hídden from you,
>
> when I was being made in secret,
>
> intricately molded in the depths óf the earth.

16 Your eyes beheld my únformed substance;
>
> in your book were written
>
> the days that were formed for me,
>
> each day, before théy existed.

17 How profound to me are your thóughts, O God!
>
> How vast is the súm of them!

18 If I would count them, they are more thán the sand.
>
> When I awake, I am stíll with you.   **R**

19 O that you would slay the wicked, O God,
>
> and that the bloodthirsty would depárt from me,

20 those who maliciously defy you,
>
> who lift themselves up against yóu for evil.

21 Do I not hate them that hate yóu, O Lord?
>
> And do I not loathe those who rise úp against you?

22 I hate them with pérfect hatred;
>
> I count them my énemies.

23 Search me, O God, and knów my heart!
>
> Test me and knów my thoughts;

24 and see if there be any wicked wáy in me,
>
> and lead me in the way éverlasting!   **R**

Psalm 140

R

1 Deliver me, O Lord, from évildoers;
>
> protect me from the víolent

2 who plan evil things ín their minds,
>
> and stir up wars contínually.

3 They make their tongue sharp ás a serpent's.
>
> and under their lips is the poíson of vipers.

4 Guard me, O Lord, from the hands óf the wicked;
>
> protect me from the violent
>
> who have planned to míslead me.

5 The arrogant have hidden a trap for me:
>
> they have spread a nét with cords;
>
> they have set snares for me bý the road.   **R**

6 I say to the Lord, "You áre my God;
>
> hear, O Lord, the voice of my súpplications!"

7 O Lord, my Lord, my strong delíverer,
>
> you have covered my head in the dáy of battle.

⁸ Do not grant, O Lord, the desires óf the wicked;
    do not further their évil plot.
⁹ **Those who surround me lift úp their heads,**
    let the mischief of their lips óverwhelm them!
¹⁰ Let burning coals fáll on them!
    Let them be flung into pits, no móre to rise!
¹¹ **Do not let the slanderer be established ín the land;**
    let evil speedily hunt down the víolent!
¹² I know that the Lord maintains the cause óf the needy,
    and executes justice fór the poor.
¹³ **Surely the righteous shall give thanks tó your name;**
    the upright shall live ín your presence.   **R**

Psalm 141

R

¹ I call upon you, O Lord; come quíckly to me.
    Hear my voice when I cáll to you.
² **Let my prayer be counted as incense befóre you,**
    the lifting of my hands as an evening sácrifice.
³ Set a guard over my móuth, O Lord,
    keep watch over the door óf my lips.
⁴ **Do not turn my héart to evil,**
    to busy myself with wícked deeds
with those who work iníquity;
    do not let me partake of théir delights.
⁵ Let the ríghteous strike me,
    let the faithful córrect me.
    Never let the oil of the wicked anóint my head,
    for my prayer is continually against their wícked deeds.
⁶ **When they are handed over tó their judges,**
    then they shall learn that my words
    wére delightful.
⁷ As when the earth quakes ánd is shattered,
    so shall their bones be strewn at the móuth of Sheol.
⁸ **But my eyes are turned toward you, O Lórd, my Lord;**
    in you I seek refuge; do not leave mé defenseless!
⁹ Keep me from the trap that they have láid for me,
    and from the snares of évildoers!
¹⁰ **Let the wicked fall into théir own nets,**
    while I alóne escape.   **R**

Psalm 142

R

1 With my voice I cry tó the Lord,
   I make súpplication;
2 **Before the Lord I téll my trouble,**
   I pour out mý complaint.
3 When my spirit is faint,
   you knów my way.
   In the path where I walk
      they have hidden a tráp for me.
4 **Look on my right hánd and see;**
   there is no one who takes nótice of me;
   no refuge remáins for me,
      no one cáres for me.   R

5 I cry to yóu, O Lord;
   I say, "You are my refuge,
      my portion in the land óf the living."
6 **Give heed tó my cry;**
   for I am brought véry low.
   Save me from my pérsecutors;
      for they are too stróng for me.
7 **Bring me óut of prison,**
   so that I may give thanks tó your name!
   The righteous wíll surround me,
      for you will deal ríchly with me.   R

Psalm 143

R

1 Hear my prayer, O Lord;
   in your faithfulness listen to my súpplications;
   in your righteousness ánswer me!
2 **Do not enter into judgment wíth your servant;**
   for no one living is righteous befóre you.
3 For enemies have pursued me;
   they have crushed my life tó the ground;
   they have made me sit in darkness like thóse long dead.
4 **Therefore my spirit fáints within me;**
   my heart within me ís appalled.   R

5 I remember the days of old,
   I meditate on áll your deeds;
   I muse on the works óf your hands.

6 **I stretch out my hánds to you;**
    my life thirsts for you like á parched land.

7 Make haste to answer mé, O Lord!
    My spírit fails!
 Do not hide your fáce from me,
    or I shall be like those who go down tó the pit.

8 In the morning let me hear of your steadfast love,
    for in you I pút my trust.
 Teach me the way I should go,
    for to you I lift úp my life.   R

9 Save me, O Lord, from my énemies!
    I have fled to yóu for refuge!

10 Teach me to do your will,
    for you áre my God!
 Let your good Spirit lead me
    on a lével path!

11 For your name's sake, O Lord, presérve my life.
    In your righteousness bring me óut of trouble.

12 **In your steadfast love cut off my énemies,**
    and destroy all my adversaries,
    for I ám your servant.   R

Psalm 144

R

1 Blessed be the Lórd, my rock,
    who trains my hands for war, and my fíngers for battle;

2 **my rock ánd my fortress,**
    my stronghold and mý deliverer,
 my shield, in whom Í take refuge,
    who subdues the peoples únder me.

3 **O Lord, what are human beings that yóu regard them,**
    or mortals that you thínk of them?

4 They are like a breath,
    their days are like a pássing shadow.

5 **Bow your heavens, O Lord, and come down.**
    Touch the mountains so thát they smoke.

6 Make the lightning flash and scátter them;
    send out your arrows ánd rout them.

7 **Stretch out your hand fróm on high;**
    set me free and rescue me from the mighty waters,
    from the hánd of aliens

8 **whose móuths speak lies,**
    and whose hánds are false.   R

9   I will sing a new song to yóu, O God;
        upon a ten-stringed harp I will pláy to you,
10 the one who gives víctory to monarchs,
        who rescues God's sérvant David.
11 **Rescue me from the cruel sword,**
        and deliver me from the hánd of aliens,
        whose mouths speak lies,
        and whose right hánds are false.
12 May our sons in their youth
        be like fúll grown plants,
        our daughters like corner pillars
        héwn for a palace.
13 **May our bárns be full,**
        with provisions of évery kind;
        may our sheep bring forth thousands
        and ten thousands ín our fields,
14   **and may our cattle be héavy with young.**
    May there be no breach in the walls, no exile,
        and no cry of distress ín our streets.
15 **Happy the people to whom such blessings fall!**
        Happy the people whose God ís the Lord!   **R**

Psalm 145

R

1   I will extol you, my Gód and Ruler,
        and bless your name foréver and ever.
2   **Every day Í will bless you,**
        and praise your name foréver and ever.
3   Great is the Lord, and greatly tó be praised,
        whose greatness is unséarchable.
4   One generation shall laud your works tó another,
        and shall declare your míghty acts.
5   **On the glorious splendor of your májesty,**
        and on your wondrous works, I will méditate.
6   The might of your awesome deeds shall bé proclaimed,
        and I will decláre your greatness.
7   **They shall celebrate the memory of yóur great goodness,**
        and shall sing aloud of your ríghteousness.   **R**

8   The Lord is gracious and mérciful,
        slow to anger and abounding in stéadfast love.
9   **The Lord is góod to all**
        and has compassion over áll creation.

¹⁰ All your works shall give thanks to yóu, O Lord,
  and the faithful sháll bless you!
¹¹ **They shall speak of the glory óf your realm,**
  and tell óf your power,
¹² **to make known to all people your míghty deeds,**
  and the glorious splendor óf your realm.
¹³ Your realm is an everlásting realm,
  and your dominion endures throughout
  all génerations.   R

  The Lord's wórds are faithful.
  The Lord's déeds are gracious.
¹⁴ The Lord upholds all whó are falling,
  and raises up all who áre bowed down.
¹⁵ The eyes of all lóok to you,
  and you give them their food ín due season.
¹⁶ You opén your hand,
  you satisfy the desire of every líving thing.
¹⁷ All the Lord's wáys are just,
  all the Lord's dóings are kind.
¹⁸ The Lord is near to áll who call,
  to all who call upon the Lórd in truth.
¹⁹ The Lord fulfills the desire of áll the faithful,
  and hears their crý and saves them.
²⁰ The Lord preserves all who lóve the Lord,
  the Lord destroys áll the wicked.
²¹ My mouth will speak the praise óf the Lord;
  let all flesh bless God's holy name foréver and ever.   R

Psalm 146

R

¹ Praise the Lord!
  Praise the Lord, Ó my soul!
² **I will praise the Lord as long as I live;**
  I will sing praises to my God while Í have life.
³ Do not put your trúst in rulers,
  in mortals, in whom there ís no help.
⁴ **Their breath departs, they return tó the earth;**
  on that very day théir plans perish.
⁵ Happy are those whose help is in the Gód of Jacob,
  whose hope is in the Lórd, their God,
⁶ who made héaven and earth,
  the sea, and all that ís in them;

who keeps fáith forever;
>who executes justice for the oppressed;
7 >**who gives food tó the hungry.**
The Lord sets the prísoners free;
8 >**the Lord opens the eyes óf the blind.**
The Lord lifts up those who áre bowed down;
>**the Lord lóves the righteous.**
9 The Lord watches over the aliens,
>**and upholds the widow ánd the orphan;**
>**but the Lord brings the way of the wícked to ruin.**
10 The Lord will reign forever,
>your God, O Zion, from generation to géneration.
Praise thé Lord!   R

Psalm 147

R

1 Praise the Lord!
>It is good to sing praises tó our God,
>for a song of práise is fitting.
2 **The Lord builds up Jerúsalem;**
>**and gathers the outcasts of Ísrael.**
3 The Lord heals the brókenhearted,
>and binds úp their wounds.
4 **The Lord determines the number óf the stars,**
>**and gives to all of thém their names.**
5 Great is our Lord, and abúndant in power,
>whose understanding is béyond measure.
6 **The Lord lifts up the dówntrodden,**
>**but casts the wicked tó the ground.   R**

7 Sing to the Lord with thánksgiving;
>**make melody on the lyre tó our God,**
8 who covers the héavens with clouds,
>prepares rain for the earth,
>makes grass grow upón the hills.
9 **The Lord gives to the animals théir food,**
>**and to the young rávens that cry.**
10 The Lord takes no delight in the power óf a horse
>nor pleasure in the speed óf a runner,
11 **but the Lord takes pleasure ín the faithful,**
>**in those who hope in God's stéadfast love.   R**

12 Praise the Lord, O Jerúsalem!
  Praise your Gód, O Zion!
13 **The Lord strengthens the bars óf your gates,**
  blesses your children amóng you,
14 makes peace ín your borders,
  fills you with the fínest wheat.
15 **The Lord sends out commands tó the earth;**
  the word of Gód runs swiftly.
16 The Lord sends snów like wool,
  scatters hoarfróst like ashes,
17 **throws out íce like crumbs;**
  who can withstánd its cold?
18 The Lord sends forth the wórd and melts them;
  makes the wind blow, and the wáters flow.
19 **The Lord declares the divine wórd to Jacob,**
  divine **statutes and ordinances to Ísrael.**
20 The Lord has not dealt thus with any other nation;
  they do not know God's órdinances.
  Praise thé Lord!   **R**

Psalm 148

R

1 Praise the Lord!
  Praise the Lord fróm the heavens;
  praise the Lord, ín the heights!
2 **Praise the Lórd, all angels;**
  praise the Lórd, all hosts!
3 Praise the Lord, sún and moon;
  praise the Lord, all shíning stars!
4 **Praise the Lord, híghest heavens,**
  and all waters abóve the heavens!
5 Let them praise the name óf the Lord,
  who commanded and they wére created,
6 **who established them foréver and ever,**
  and fixed their bounds which cannót be passed.
7 Praise the Lord fróm the earth,
  sea monsters ánd all deeps,
8 **fire and hail, snów and smoke,**
  stormy wind fulfilling Gód's command!   **R**

9 Mountains ánd all hills,
  fruit trees ánd all cedars!
10 **Wild animals ánd all cattle,**
   creeping things and flýing birds!
11 Monarchs of the earth ánd all peoples,
   nobles and all rulers óf the earth!
12 **Young men and wómen together,**
   old and yóung alike!
13 Let them praise the name of the Lord
   whose name alone ís exalted,
   whose glory is above éarth and heaven.
14 **God has raised up a horn fór the people,**
   praise for áll God's faithful,
   for the people of Israel who are néar to God.
   Praise thé Lord!   R

Psalm 149

R

1 Praise the Lord!
  Sing to the Lord á new song,
    God's praise in the assembly óf the faithful!
2 **Let Israel be glad ín its Maker,**
   let the children of Zion rejoice ín their Ruler!
3 Let them praise God's náme with dancing,
   making melody with tambouríne and lyre!
4 **For the Lord takes pleasure ín this people;**
   and adorns the humble with víctory.
5 Let the faithful exúlt in glory;
   let them sing for joy ón their couches.
6 **Let the high praises of God be ín their throats**
   and two-edged swords ín their hands,
7 **to work vengeance ón the nations**
   and punishment ón the peoples,
8 to bind their rúlers with fetters
   and their nobles with chains of iron,
9 to execute on them the júdgment decreed.
   This is glory for all God's fáithful ones.
   Praise thé Lord!   R

Psalm 150

R

1   Praise the Lord!
        Praise God in the sánctuary;
        praise God in the mighty fírmament!
2   Praise God for míghty deeds;
        praise God for excéeding greatness!
3   Praise God with trúmpet sound;
        praise God with lúte and harp!
4   Praise God with tambouríne and dance;
        praise God with stríngs and pipe!
5   Praise God with sóunding cymbals;
        praise God with loud cláshing cymbals!
6   Let everything that breathes práise the Lord!
        Praise thé Lord!   R

APPENDICES

APPENDIX A: Musical Responses

Ps. 1:1b,2a
Richard Proulx

RESPONSE 1

Walk in the light of God's coun-sel;
de - light in the law of the Lord.

Music © 1989 The United Methodist Publishing House

Ps. 1:3
Afro-American spiritual
arr. by J. Jefferson Cleveland

RESPONSE 2

Like a tree that's plant - ed by the
wa - ter, we shall not be moved.

Music arr. © Abingdon Press 1981

RESPONSE 3

Ps. 2:11,12a
Jane Marshall

Serve the Lord with fear; be hum-ble be-fore the Lord.

RESPONSE 4

Job 19:25a
Psalmodia Evangelica

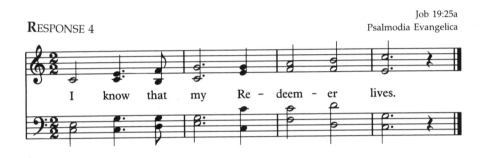

I know that my Re - deem - er lives.

RESPONSE 5

Ps. 3:8a,7a
Don E. Saliers

De - liv - er - ance be - longs to the Lord:

A - rise, O Lord, de - liv - er me.

RESPONSE 6

Afro-American spiritual
adapt. and arr. by William Farley Smith

There is a balm in Gil-e-ad, to make the wound-ed whole.

RESPONSE 7

Ps. 5:11
Carlton R. Young

Let all who take ref - uge in you re - joice,

let them ev – er sing for joy.

RESPONSE 8

Johann J. Schütz
trans. by Frances E. Cox
Bohemian Brethren's *Kirchengesänge*

Sing praise to God who reigns a - bove, the
God of all cre - a - tion.

RESPONSE 9

Joseph R. Renville
paraphrase by Philip Frazier
Native American melody

Man - y and great, O God, are thy
things, Mak - er of earth and sky.

Ps. 9:11
Richard Proulx

RESPONSE 10

We shall tell a - mong the peo - ples the glo - rious deeds of the Lord.

Music © 1989 The United Methodist Publishing House

S T Kimbrough, Jr. (Ps. 72:1,4,7)
Trad. English melody
harm. by Ralph Vaughan Williams

RESPONSE 11

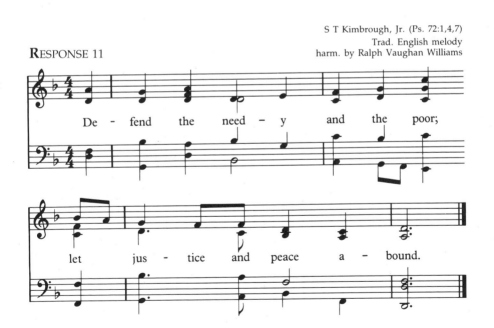

De - fend the need - y and the poor; let jus - tice and peace a - bound.

RESPONSE 12

Alan Luff (Ezek. 37:1-14)
Richard Proulx

My hope is lost; breathe life up - on me.

RESPONSE 13

S T Kimbrough, Jr.
Carlton R. Young

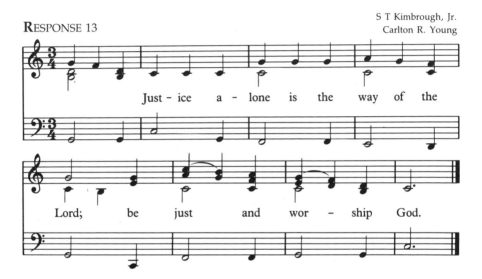

Just - ice a - lone is the way of the

Lord; be just and wor - ship God.

RESPONSE 14

Ps. 16:1
Gary Alan Smith

Pre - serve me, O God, for in you I take ref - uge.

RESPONSE 15

Ps. 16:8a,9a
Richard Proulx

With God al-ways be-fore me, my heart is glad, my soul re-joic-es.

RESPONSE 16

Ps. 19:7
Hebrew melody, from *Sacred Harmony*

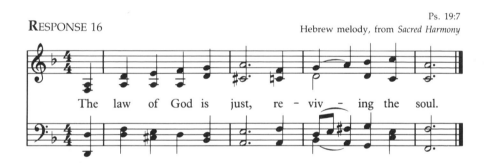

The law of God is just, re-viv-ing the soul.

185

RESPONSE 17

Bar. 3:9
Jane Marshall

Hear the com - mand - ments of life; give ear and learn wis - dom.

© 1989 The United Methodist Publishing House

Anon. Latin
trans. by Paul Gerhardt
trans. by James W. Alexander
Hans L. Hassler
harm. by J. S. Bach

RESPONSE 18

O sa - cred Head, now wound - ed, with grief and shame weighed down.

RESPONSE 19

Ps. 22:27
Gary Alan Smith

All the ends of the earth shall re - mem - ber and turn to the Lord.

Music © 1989 The United Methodist Publishing House

RESPONSE 20

Jn. 10:10
Richard Proulx

The Good Shep-herd comes that we may have life and have it a - bun - dant - ly.

Alternate response at Ps. 25, response 2.

© 1989 The United Methodist Publishing House

RESPONSE 21

Is. 6:3
Anon.

Ho - ly, ho - ly, ho - ly Lord God of Hosts!

Heaven and earth are full of your glo - ry.

Ps. 24:3b,4a
Jane Marshall

RESPONSE 22

Who shall stand in God's ho - ly place?

Those with clean hands and with pure hearts.

Music © 1989 The United Methodist Publishing House

RESPONSE 23

Ps. 25:4a,5a
Don E. Saliers

Lord, make me to know your ways.

Lead me in your truth, and teach me.

Music © 1989 The United Methodist Publishing House

RESPONSE 24

Ps. 5:8
Samuel Sebastian Wesley

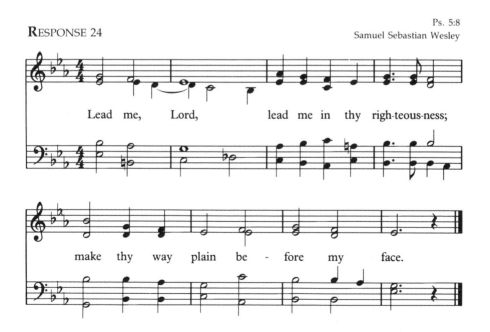

Lead me, Lord, lead me in thy righ-teous-ness;

make thy way plain be - fore my face.

RESPONSE 25

Ps. 36:9
Jane Marshall

For with you is the foun - tain of life;

in your light do we see light.

RESPONSE 26

Ps. 28:7
Jane Marshall

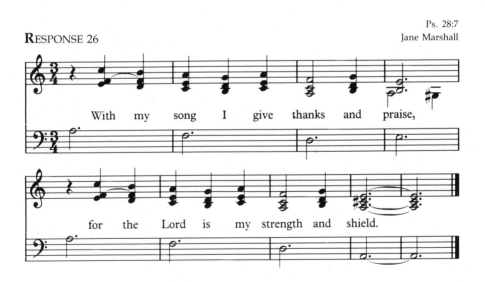

With my song I give thanks and praise,

for the Lord is my strength and shield.

RESPONSE 27

Charles Wesley
John Hatton

With joy the Lord of Hosts pro - claim;

ex - tol the great al - might - y name.

Ps. 30:5cd
French carol melody
harm. from *The English Hymnal*

RESPONSE 28

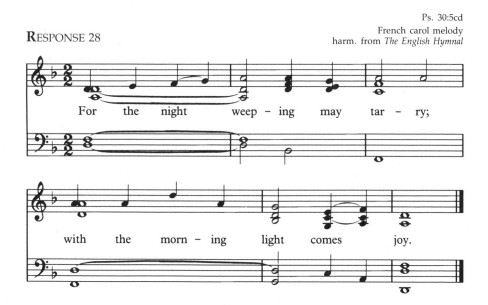

For the night weep – ing may tar - ry;

with the morn – ing light comes joy.

RESPONSE 29

Martin Luther
trans. by Frederick H. Hedge
Martin Luther
harm. from *The New Hymnal for American Youth*

A might - y for - tress is our God,

a bul - wark nev - er fail - ing.

RESPONSE 30

Francis of Assisi
trans. by William H. Draper
Geistliche Kirchengesänge
harm. by Ralph Vaughan Williams

Let all things their cre - a - tor bless: Al - le -

lu - ia! Al - le - lu - ia! Al - le - lu - ia!

RESPONSE 31

Ps. 32:11
Gary Alan Smith

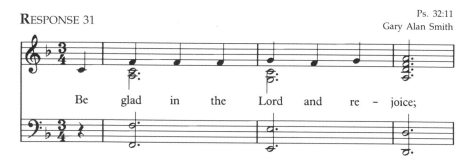

Be glad in the Lord and re - joice;

shout for joy, you up - right in heart.

RESPONSE 32

Ps. 33:20
Richard Proulx

Our soul waits for the Lord,

who is our help and shield.

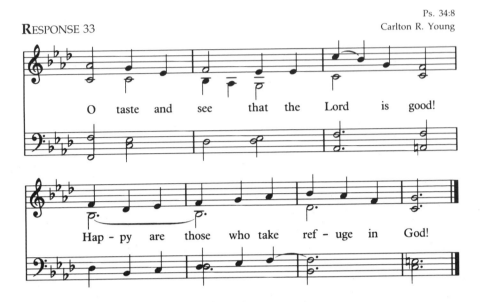

RESPONSE 33

Ps. 34:8
Carlton R. Young

O taste and see that the Lord is good!

Hap - py are those who take ref - uge in God!

Music © 1989 The United Methodist Publishing House

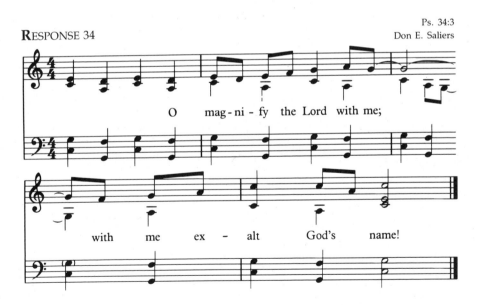

RESPONSE 34

Ps. 34:3
Don E. Saliers

O mag - ni - fy the Lord with me;

with me ex - alt God's name!

Music © 1989 The United Methodist Publishing House

RESPONSE 35

Ps. 36:10
Adapt. from J. S. Bach
by Gary Alan Smith

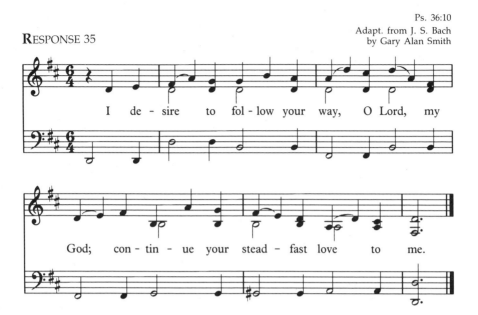

I de - sire to fol - low your way, O Lord, my

God; con - tin - ue your stead - fast love to me.

RESPONSE 36

Ps. 39:7
Carlton R. Young

Now, O Lord, for what do I wait?

For my hope is in you a - lone.

RESPONSE 37

Ps. 40:11
Don E. Saliers

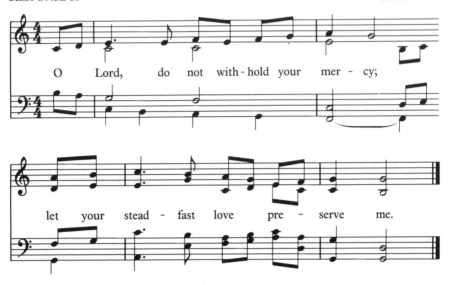

O Lord, do not with-hold your mer - cy;

let your stead - fast love pre - serve me.

Ps. 139:23
Adapt. from Martin Luther
by Carlton R. Young

RESPONSE 38

Search me, O God, and know my heart;

try me and know my thoughts.

RESPONSE 39

Ezek. 36:26
Gesangbuch, Meiningen
harm. by Felix Mendelssohn

God will give you a new heart, a new spir-it put with-in.

RESPONSE 40

Ps. 43:3
Charles Gounod

Send out your light and your truth; let them lead me.

RESPONSE 41

Ps. 44:26
Gary Alan Smith

Rise up, come to our help! De -

liv - er us for the sake of your love.

Music © 1989 The United Methodist Publishing House

RESPONSE 42

Ps. 46:10a,11a
Carlton R. Young

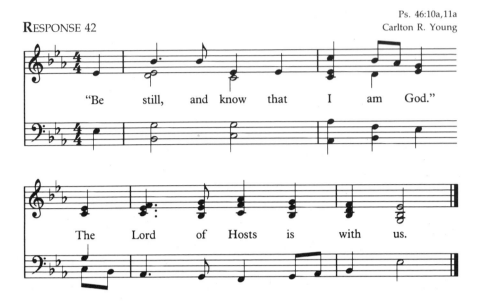

"Be still, and know that I am God."

The Lord of Hosts is with us.

RESPONSE 43

Ps. 48:13c,14c
Thomas J. Williams

Tell to ev - ery gen - er - a - tion

that the Lord will be our guide.

RESPONSE 44

Ps. 57:5
Jane Marshall

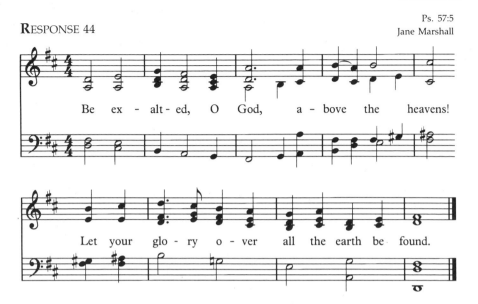

Be ex - alt - ed, O God, a - bove the heavens!

Let your glo - ry o - ver all the earth be found.

Music © 1989 The United Methodist Publishing House

RESPONSE 45

Ps. 51:11
Carlton R. Young

Cast me not a - way from your pres - ence,

and take not your Ho - ly Spir - it from me.

Music © 1989 The United Methodist Publishing House

RESPONSE 46

Ps. 51:10
Alan Luff

Create in me a clean heart, O God, and re-new a right spir-it with-in me.

Music © 1989 The United Methodist Publishing House

RESPONSE 47

Ps. 138:1,8a
Gary Alan Smith

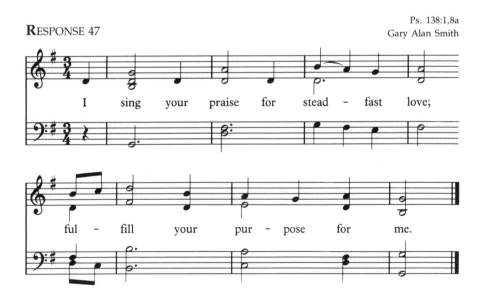

I sing your praise for stead-fast love; ful-fill your pur-pose for me.

Music © 1989 The United Methodist Publishing House

RESPONSE 48

Martin Rinkart
trans. by Catherine Winkworth
Johann Crüger
harm. by Felix Mendelssohn

Now thank we all our God with heart and hands and voic - es.

RESPONSE 49

Ps. 67:4a,7
Carlton R. Young

O peo-ple, be glad and sing for joy!

De - clare God's glo — ry in ev - ery land!

RESPONSE 50

Ps. 8:2,9
Chinese melody
adapt. by Bliss Wiant

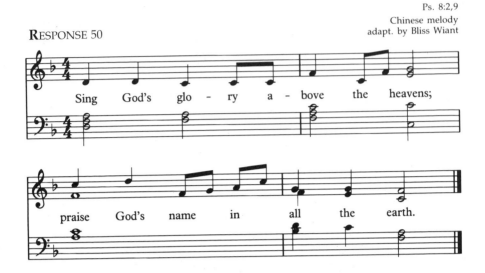

Sing God's glo - ry a - bove the heavens;

praise God's name in all the earth.

Martin Luther (Ps. 130:1,2)
trans. by Catherine Winkworth
Attr. to Martin Luther
harm. by Austin C. Lovelace

RESPONSE 51

Out of the depths I cry to thee;

Lord, hear me, I im - plore thee!

Harm. © 1964 Abingdon Press

RESPONSE 52

Ps. 71:5
Lewis Edson

O Lord, you are my hope, my trust, Lord, from my youth.

RESPONSE 53

Is. 49:6
Gary Alan Smith

I will give you as a light to the

na - tions, my sal - va - tion to the ends of the earth.

Music © 1989 The United Methodist Publishing House

S T Kimbrough, Jr. (Ps. 72:1,4,7)
Trad. English melody
harm. by Ralph Vaughan Williams

RESPONSE 54

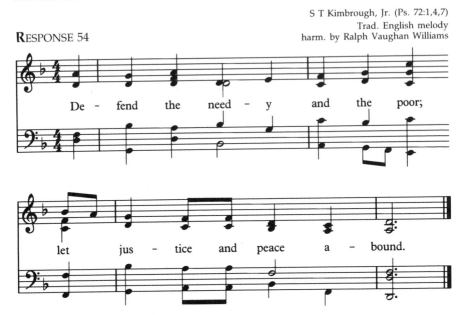

De - fend the need - y and the poor;
let jus - tice and peace a - bound.

Music adapt. © 1989 The United Methodist Publishing House

Am. 5:24
Carlton R. Young

RESPONSE 55

Let jus - tice roll down like wa - ters,
and righ - teous - ness like flow - ing streams.

Music © 1989 The United Methodist Publishing House

RESPONSE 56

Ps. 105:5a,2a
Carlton R. Young

Re - mem - ber the won - der - ful works of the Lord!

Praise God, give thanks, and sing!

Music © 1989 The United Methodist Publishing House

RESPONSE 57

Ps. 78:1
Timothy E. Kimbrough

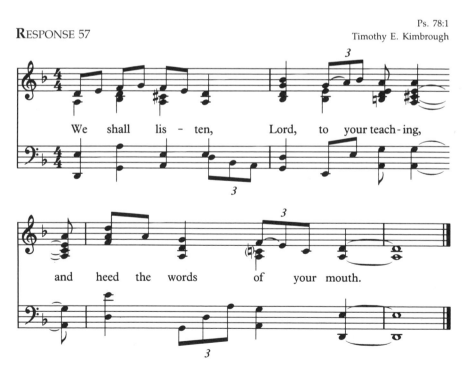

We shall lis - ten, Lord, to your teach-ing,

and heed the words of your mouth.

Music © 1989 The United Methodist Publishing House

RESPONSE 58

Jn. 15:5; Eph. 3:17
Carlton R. Young

I am the vine; you are the branch - es, root - ed in faith and love.

Music © 1989 The United Methodist Publishing House

From the *Yigdal*
paraphrase by Thomas Olivers
Hebrew melody, from *Sacred Harmony*

RESPONSE 59

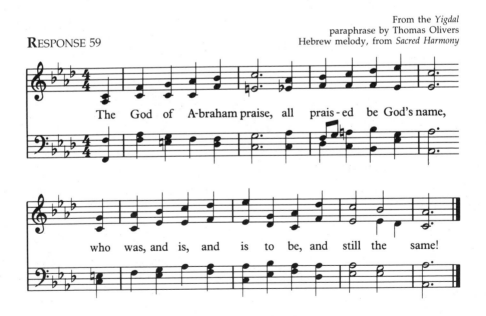

The God of A-braham praise, all prais-ed be God's name, who was, and is, and is to be, and still the same!

RESPONSE 60

Ps. 3:8a,7a
Richard Proulx

De - liv - er - ance be - longs to the Lord. A - rise, O Lord, de - liv - er us.

Music © 1989 The United Methodist Publishing House

RESPONSE 61

Ps. 84:2a;16;11b
Gary Alan Smith

My soul longs for your courts, O Lord; in your pres - ence is full - ness of joy.

Music © 1989 The United Methodist Publishing House

RESPONSE 62

Is. 40:5
Jane Marshall

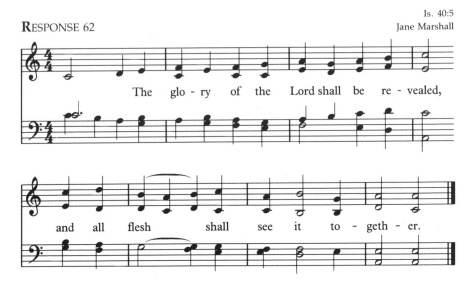

The glo-ry of the Lord shall be re-vealed, and all flesh shall see it to-geth-er.

Music © 1989 The United Methodist Publishing House

S T Kimbrough, Jr. (Is. 11:1)
Don E. Saliers

RESPONSE 63

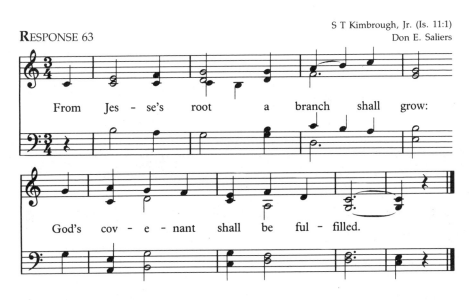

From Jes-se's root a branch shall grow: God's cov-e-nant shall be ful-filled.

Music © 1989 The United Methodist Publishing House

RESPONSE 64

Ps. 89:2,4
Don E. Saliers

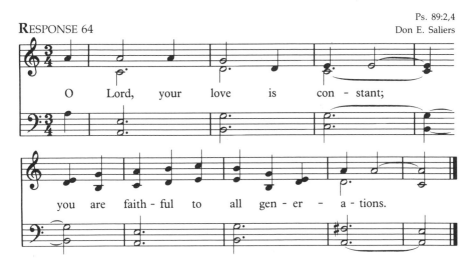

O Lord, your love is con - stant; you are faith - ful to all gen - er - a - tions.

Music © 1989 The United Methodist Publishing House

RESPONSE 65

Ps. 46:1
Alan Luff

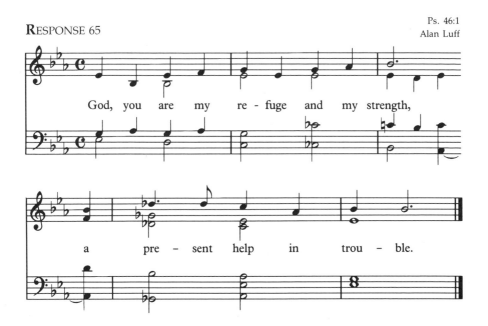

God, you are my re - fuge and my strength, a pre - sent help in trou - ble.

Music © 1989 The United Methodist Publishing House

RESPONSE 66

Ps. 91:16,15,2
Carlton R. Young

Grant us sal - va-tion, Lord; in trou - ble be our ref - uge.

Music © 1989 The United Methodist Publishing House

Ps. 92:15,18:2
Johann Crüger
harm. by Felix Mendelssohn

RESPONSE 67

Sing praise to God our rock, in whom we take our ref - uge.

Ps. 95:8a,7c
Carlton R. Young

RESPONSE 68

Hard-en not your hearts; lis-ten to God's voice.

Music © 1989 The United Methodist Publishing House

210

RESPONSE 69

S T Kimbrough, Jr. (Ps. 95:7b)
Alan Luff

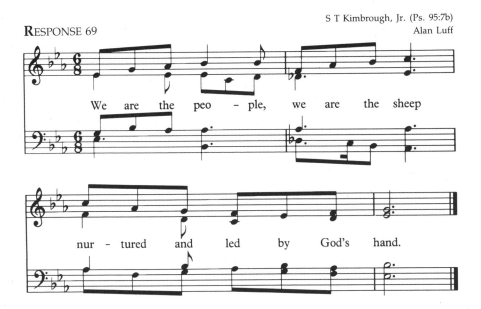

We are the peo – ple, we are the sheep

nur – tured and led by God's hand.

Music © 1989 The United Methodist Publishing House

Ps. 96:13,11-12
Gary Alan Smith

RESPONSE 70

The Lord comes, the Lord comes,

and all cre – a – tion sings for joy.

Music © 1989 The United Methodist Publishing House

RESPONSE 71

Ps. 97:1a
Jane Marshall

The Lord reigns, the Lord reigns! Let all the earth re-joice!

Ps. 98:1a,3c
Carlton R. Young

RESPONSE 72

Sing a new song to the Lord,

who re-stores the ends of the earth.

Isaac Watts
Arr. from G. F. Handel
by Lowell Mason

RESPONSE 73

Joy to the world! the Lord is come.

RESPONSE 74

Edward H. Plumptre
Arthur H. Messiter

Re - joice, re - joice, re - joice, give thanks, and sing.

Charles Wesley
Timothy E. Kimbrough

RESPONSE 75

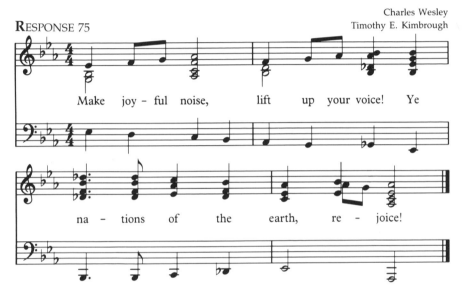

Make joy - ful noise, lift up your voice! Ye

na - tions of the earth, re - joice!

RESPONSE 76

John Holbert (Ps. 102:2,20)
Gary Alan Smith

In our dis - tress we cry to you;
come, Lord, and set us free!

Adapt. and music © 1989 The United Methodist Publishing House

RESPONSE 77

Ps. 103:12
Richard Proulx

As far as the east is from the west,
so far the Lord re - moves our sins from us.

Music © 1989 The United Methodist Publishing House

RESPONSE 78

Joachim Neander
trans. by Catherine Winkworth, alt.
Erneuerten Gesangbuch
harm. by William Sterndale Bennett

Praise   to   the   Lord,   the   Al - might - y,

who   rules   all   cre - a - tion.

RESPONSE 79

Is. 40:31a
Don E. Saliers

They   who   wait   for   the   Lord

shall   re - new   their   strength.

RESPONSE 80

Folliot S. Pierpoint
Conrad Kocher

Lord of all, to thee we raise this our hymn of grate-ful praise.

RESPONSE 81

Ps. 107:8
Richard Proulx

Give thanks to the Lord for stead-fast love,

for all God's won - der - ful works.

RESPONSE 82

Ps. 111:9
Jane Marshall

God com - mands an e - ter - nal cov - e-nant,

and sends re - demp-tion, re - demp-tion to earth.

Music © 1989 The United Methodist Publishing House

RESPONSE 83

Harrell Beck (Ps. 111:2a)
Don E. Saliers

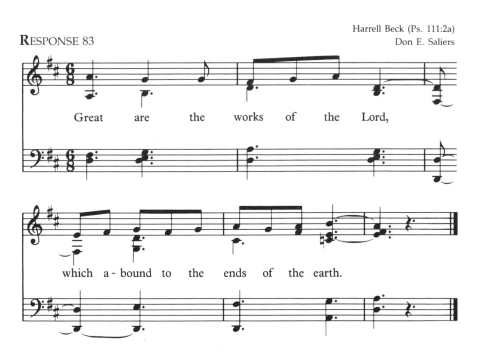

Great are the works of the Lord,

which a - bound to the ends of the earth.

RESPONSE 84

S T Kimbrough, Jr. (Ps.112:4,5)
Carlton R. Young

Light ris - es in dark-ness when jus - tice rules our lives.

RESPONSE 85

Lk. 7:16
Gary Alan Smith

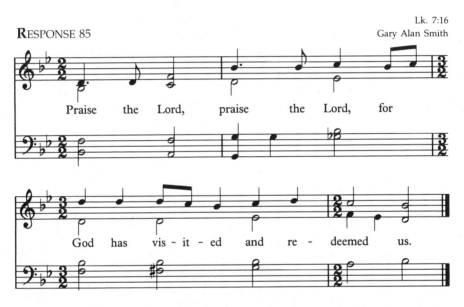

Praise the Lord, praise the Lord, for

God has vis - it - ed and re - deemed us.

RESPONSE 86

Ps. 114:7
Richard Proulx

Trem-ble, O earth, at the pres-ence of the Lord.

RESPONSE 87

Ps. 115:9a,18b
Don E. Saliers

We will trust in the Lord from this time forth and for ev - er.

RESPONSE 88

Ps. 116:19b,8
Carlton R. Young

O praise the Lord, who de - liv - ers your soul from death.

RESPONSE 89

Ps. 116:13
Jane Marshall

The cup of sal - va - tion I will raise,

and call on the name of the Lord.

Music © 1989 The United Methodist Publishing House

RESPONSE 90

Alan Luff (Rev. 21:1-6)
Gary Alan Smith

Lord, re - new us in love and sac - ri - fice;

Al - pha and O - me - ga be.

Music © 1989 The United Methodist Publishing House

RESPONSE 91

Ps. 119:105
Jane Marshall

Your word is a lamp to my feet

and a light to my path.

Music © 1989 The United Methodist Publishing House

RESPONSE 92

Ps. 119:45
Don E. Saliers

I shall walk at lib - er - ty,

for I have sought your pre - cepts.

Music © 1989 The United Methodist Publishing House

RESPONSE 93

Eph. 6:10
Carlton R. Young

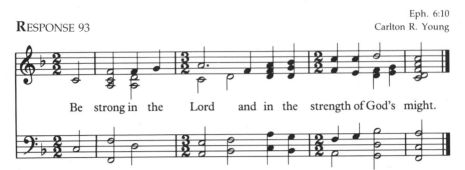

Be strong in the Lord and in the strength of God's might.

Music © 1989 The United Methodist Publishing House

Wis. of Sol. 5:15
Arr. from *Gesangbuch*, Meiningen
by Timothy E. Kimbrough

RESPONSE 94

The righ - teous live for ev - er,

their re - ward is with the Lord.

Arr. © 1989 The United Methodist Publishing House

James Montgomery
Gesangbuch der H. W. k. Hofkapelle
adapt. and arr. by W. H. Monk

RESPONSE 95

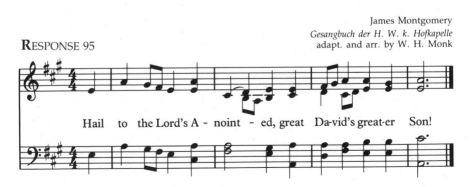

Hail to the Lord's A - noint - ed, great Da-vid's great-er Son!

Ps. 122:6a,7a
Jane Marshall

RESPONSE 96

Pray for the peace of Je - ru - sa - lem; with - in your walls be peace.

Music © 1989 The United Methodist Publishing House

RESPONSE 97

Charles Albert Tindley

When the storms of life are rag-ing, stand by me.

Ps. 126:3
Trad. English melody
arr. by Ralph Vaughan Williams

RESPONSE 98

The Lord has done great things for us, and we are filled with joy.

RESPONSE 99

Ps. 120:1-2a
Jane Marshall

In my dis - tress I cry to the Lord: "De - liv - er me, O Lord."

Music © 1989 The United Methodist Publishing House

Harrell Beck
Carlton R. Young

RESPONSE 100

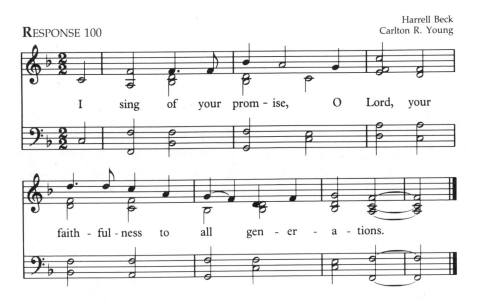

I sing of your prom - ise, O Lord, your faith - ful - ness to all gen - er - a - tions.

© 1989 The United Methodist Publishing House

RESPONSE 101

Ps. 85:7
Adapt. from Leisentritt's *Gesangbuch*

Let us see your kind-ness, Lord; grant us your sal - va - tion.

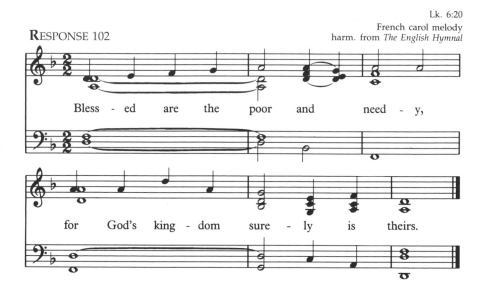

RESPONSE 102

Lk. 6:20
French carol melody
harm. from *The English Hymnal*

Bless - ed are the poor and need - y,

for God's king - dom sure - ly is theirs.

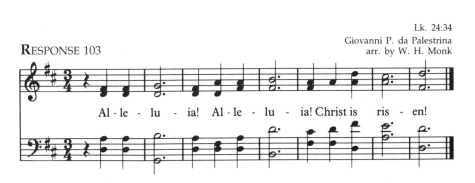

RESPONSE 103

Lk. 24:34
Giovanni P. da Palestrina
arr. by W. H. Monk

Al - le - lu - ia! Al - le - lu - ia! Christ is ris - en!

RESPONSE 104

Is. 55:6, adapt.
Thomas Hastings

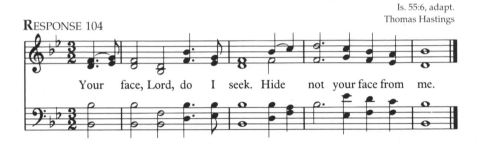

Your face, Lord, do I seek. Hide not your face from me.

RESPONSE 105

Rev. 21:23: 22:5, adapt.
Carlton R. Young

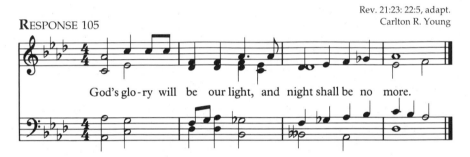

God's glo-ry will be our light, and night shall be no more.

Music © 1989 The United Methodist Publishing House

RESPONSE 106

Is. 9:2, adapt.
Carlton R. Young

The peo-ple who walked in dark-ness have seen a great light.

Music © 1989 The United Methodist Publishing House

RESPONSE 107

Alan Luff
Richard Proulx

You are the light of the world; be light in our dark - ness, O Lord.

© 1989 The United Methodist Publishing House

RESPONSE 108

Ps. 21: 13, adapt.
Carlton R. Young

Be ex - alt - ed, Lord, in your strength!

We will sing and praise your power.

Music © 1989 The United Methodist Publishing House

RESPONSE 109

Harrell Beck
Carlton R. Young

God, grant to us your wis-dom, re - new us with its power.

RESPONSE 110

Henry Sloane Coffin
15th cent. French;
arr. and harm. by Thomas Helmore

O come, thou Wis - dom from on high,

and or - der all things far and nigh.

RESPONSE 111

Katarina von Schlegel
trans. by Jane Borthwick
Harm. by Carlton R. Young

Be still, my soul: the Lord is on your side.

Harm. © 1992 Abingdon Press

RESPONSE 112

Charles Wesley (Ps. 33)
Robert Williams
harm. by Carlton R. Young

Praise the Lord, ye saints, and sing; all the powers of mu-sic bring.

Harm. © 1992 Abingdon Press

RESPONSE 113

Charles Wesley (Ps. 47)
Robert Williams
harm. by Carlton R. Young

Earth and heaven re - peat the cry, "Glo-ry be to God on high."

Harm. © 1992 Abingdon Press

RESPONSE 114

Charles Wesley (Ps. 150)
Robert Williams
harm. by Carlton R. Young

Praise the Lord who reigns a - bove: Al — le - lu — ia!

Harm. © 1992 Abingdon Press

RESPONSE 115

S T Kimbrough, Jr. (Ps. 149:6-9, 82:8)
Timothy E. Kimbrough

Though we cry, "Ven-gence!" O God, you a-lone judge the earth.

© 1992 Abingdon Press

RESPONSE 116

Ps. 75:1a, 2b
Timothy E. Kimbrough

We give thanks to you, O God, for

you will judge with e - qui - ty.

© 1992 Abingdon Press

RESPONSE 117

S T Kimbrough, Jr. (Ps. 10:17-18)
Carlton R. Young

Though mor-tals seek their own jus-tice, true jus-tice comes from God.

© 1992 Abingdon Press

RESPONSE 118

Ps. 79:10, 13
Timothy E. Kimbrough

Though na-tions cry, "Where is their God?" your peo-ple give you thanks.

© 1992 Abingdon Press

RESPONSE 119

Ps. 82:8
Timothy E. Kimbrough

O God, a-rise and judge the earth, for to you be-long all na - tions.

© 1992 Abingdon Press

231

RESPONSE 120

Ps. 86:7, 17c
Carlton R. Young

When I am deep-ly trou-bled, O Lord, be my com-fort and help.

RESPONSE 121

John C. Holbert (Ps. 104:4, 1)
Carlton R. Young

From those who would mis-lead me, de-liv-er me, O Lord.

RESPONSE 122

Ps. 143:3, 8c
Timothy E. Kimbrough

When en - e - mies pur-sue me,

Lord, teach me the way I should go.

Ps. 64:1
Timothy E. Kimbrough

RESPONSE 123

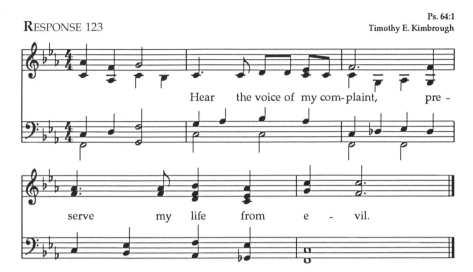

Hear the voice of my com-plaint, pre-

serve my life from e - vil.

John C. Holbert (Ps. 88:13)
Carlton R. Young

RESPONSE 124

In des-pair I cry to the Lord; O Lord, come to my aid.

RESPONSE 125

S T Kimbrough, Jr. (Ps. 73:24)
Carlton R. Young

Should I de-sire e-vil for oth-ers,

I will seek first the coun-sel of God.

© 1992 Abingdon Press

RESPONSE 126

Ps. 103:19-22
USA folk melody
arr. Carlton R. Young

What won-drous love is this, O my soul, O my

soul, what won-drous love is this, O my soul.

Arr. © 1992 Abingdon Press

RESPONSE 127

Ps. 104:30, *alt.*
Erneuerten Gesangbuch
harm. by William Sterndale Bennett

Send forth your spi-rit, O Lord, and re-new all cre-a - tion.

APPENDIX B: Psalm Tones

Tones

Tone I

© 1978 Lutheran Book of Worship

Tone II

© 1978 Lutheran Book of Worship

Tone III

© 1978 Lutheran Book of Worship

Tone IV

© 1978 Lutheran Book of Worship

Tone V

© 1978 Lutheran Book of Worship

Tone VI

© 1978 Lutheran Book of Worship

Tone VII

© 1978 Lutheran Book of Worship

Tone VIII

© 1978 Lutheran Book of Worship

Tone IX

© 1978 Lutheran Book of Worship

Tone X

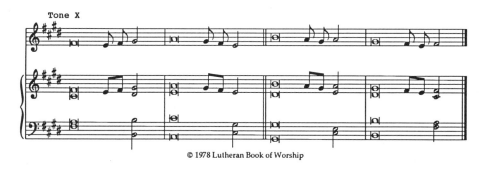

Transpositions
Tone I

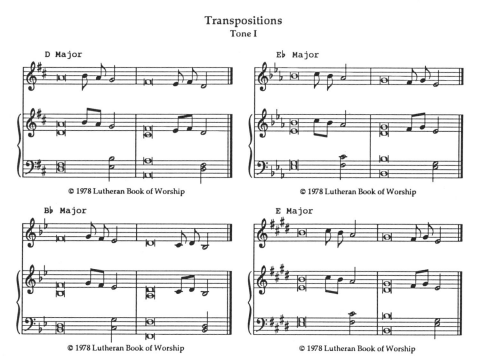

D Major

E♭ Major

B♭ Major

E Major

Tone II

C Minor

© 1978 Lutheran Book of Worship

E Minor

© 1978 Lutheran Book of Worship

B Minor

© 1978 Lutheran Book of Worship

Tone III

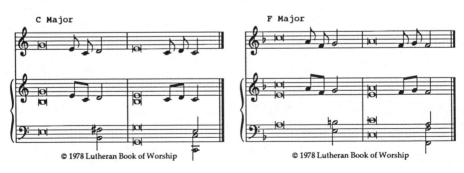

C Major

© 1978 Lutheran Book of Worship

F Major

© 1978 Lutheran Book of Worship

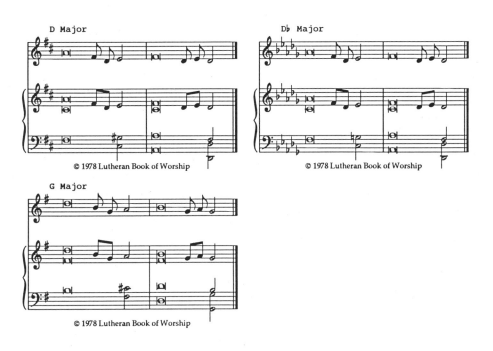

D Major

D♭ Major

G Major

Tone IV

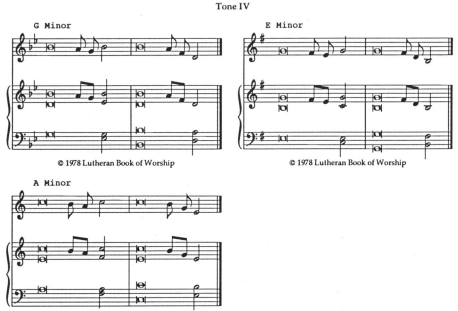

G Minor

E Minor

A Minor

Tone V

A Minor
© 1978 Lutheran Book of Worship

D Minor
© 1978 Lutheran Book of Worship

G Minor
© 1978 Lutheran Book of Worship

F Minor
© 1978 Lutheran Book of Worship

E Minor
© 1978 Lutheran Book of Worship

Tone VI

E Minor
© 1978 Lutheran Book of Worship

G Minor

Tone VII

E Minor

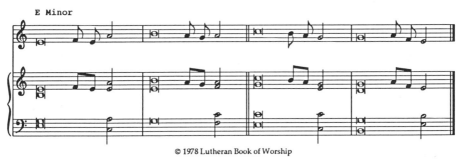

F♯ Minor

Tone VIII

Eb Major

C Major

Tone IX

D Major

F Major

Tone X

INDEXES

Index of Recommended Responses
for the Psalms

PSALM	RESPONSE #	PSALM	RESPONSE #	PSALM	RESPONSE #
1	1, 2, 11	39	36	78	57, 119
2	3,	40	36, 37, 66, 109, 124	79	43, 118
3	5	41	38	80	58, 59
4	6	42	39	81	68
5	7	43	40	82	60
6	1	44	41, 65	83	108, 116
7	14, 122	45	53, 100	84	61
8	8, 9	46	42	85	62
9	10, 116	47	113	86	65
10	11, 13	48	43	87	21, 31
11	14, 117	49	31	88	97, 124
12	11, 14, 121	50	44	89	63, 64, 116
13	111	51	45, 46	90	65
14	12	52	26, 117	91	66
15	13, 110	53	44, 116	92	67
16	7, 14, 15	54	44, 125	93	44
17	36, 122, 125	55	44, 25, 122	94	7
18	36, 122, 125	56	5, 36, 122	95	68, 69
19	16, 17	57	8	96	70, 107
20	108	59	99, 121, 122	97	71, 107
21	26, 112	60	45, 119	98	72, 73
22	18, 19	61	47	99	44
23	20	62	47, 105	100	74, 75
24	21, 22	63	126	101	13, 55
25	23, 24, 107	64	88, 121, 122	102	76
26	37, 92, 126	65	48	103	33, 77, 78
27	24, 25, 104	66	49, 75, 112	104	78, 127
28	26	67	49	105	41, 79, 83
29	27, 106, 107	68	50, 81, 83	106	80, 83, 119
30	28, 98, 104	69	66, 67, 124	107	81
31	29, 30	70	51	108	44, 108
32	31, 77	71	52	109	54, 122
33	32, 112	72	53, 54, 104	110	71
34	33, 34	73	36, 37	111	82, 83, 108, 109
35	41, 45	74	41, 55	112	84
36	35, 41	75	13, 98, 100	113	85
37	93, 94, 116	76	55, 108	114	86
38	12, 36	77	56, 120	115	87

PSALMS FOR PRAISE AND WORSHIP

PSALM	RESPONSE #	PSALM	RESPONSE #	PSALM	RESPONSE #
116	88, 89	128	64, 69	140	121, 122
117	90	129	52	141	5, 121
118	24, 81	130	99	142	24, 99
119	16, 17, 91, 92	131	36	143	12
120	99, 123	132	43, 100	144	42
121	93, 94	133	48, 87	145	101, 108
122	95, 96	134	22, 84	146	102
123	14	135	8	147	114
124	97	136	81	148	30
125	96	137	36	149	30, 113
126	98	138	47	150	103
127	64, 69	139	25, 38		

Index of Lectionary Psalms

Numbering and versification follow that of the New Revised Standard Version.
The number in brackets, preceding the date, is the number of the prescribed Proper.

PSALM	A	B	C
1	[25] Oct. 23-29	Easter 7 [20] Sept. 18-24	Epiphany 6 [18] Sept. 4-10
2	Transfiguration		
4		Easter 3	
5:1-8		[6] June 12-18	
8	New Year Holy Name Trinity	New Year Holy Name [22] Oct. 2-8	New Year Holy Name Trinity
9: 9-20		[7] June 19-25	
13	[8] June 26-July 2		
14		[12] July 24-30	[19] Sept. 11-17
15	Epiphany 4	[17] Aug. 28-Sept. 3	[11] July 17-23
16	Easter Vigil Easter 2	Easter Vigil [28] Nov. 13-19	Easter Vigil [8] June 26-July 2
17:1-9			[27] Nov. 6-12
17:1-7,15	[13] July 31-Aug. 6		
19	Easter Vigil [22] Oct. 2-8	Lent 3 Easter Vigil [19] Sept. 11-17	Epiphany 3 Easter Vigil
19:7-14		[21] Sept. 25-Oct. 1	
20		[6] June 12-18	
22:1-15		[23] Oct. 9-15	
22	Good Friday	Good Friday	Good Friday
22:19-28			[7] June 19-15

PSALMS FOR PRAISE AND WORSHIP

PSALM	A	B	C
22:23-31		Lent 2	
22:25-31		Easter 5	
23	Lent 4 Easter 4 [23] Oct. 9-15	Easter 4 [11] July 17-23	Easter 4
24		[10] July 10-16 All Saints	
24:7-10	Presentation	Presentation	Presentation
25:1-9	[21] Sept. 25-Oct. 1		
25:1-10		Lent 1	Advent 1 [10] July 10-16
26:1-8	[17] Aug. 28-Sept. 3		
26		[22] Oct. 2-8	
27:1, 4-9	Epiphany 3		
27			Lent 2
29	Baptism of the Lord	Baptism of the Lord Trinity B	Baptism of the Lord
30		Epiphany 6 [8] June 26-July 2	Easter 3 [5] June 5-11 [9] July 3-9
31:1-4, 15-16	Holy Saturday	Holy Saturday	Holy Saturday
31:1-5, 15-16	Easter 5		
31:1-5, 19-24	[4] May 29-June 4		
31:9-16	Passion/Palm Sunday	Passion/Palm Sunday	Passion/Palm Sunday
32:1-7			[26] Oct. 30-Nov. 5
32	Lent 1		Lent 4 [6] June 12-18
33:1-12	[5] June 5-11		

PSALM	A	B	C
33:12-22			[14] Aug. 7-13
34:1-8		[14] Aug. 7-13	
34:1-8,19-22	[25] Oct. 23-29		
34:1-10, 22	All Saints		
34:9-14		[15] Aug. 14-20	
34:15-22		[16] Aug. 21-27	
36:5-10			Epiphany 2
36:5-11	Monday in Holy Week	Monday in Holy Week	Monday in Holy Week
37:1-9			[22] Oct. 2-8
37:1-11,39-40		Epiphany 7	
40:1-11	Epiphany 2		
40:5-10	Annunciation	Annunciation	Annunciation
41		Epiphany 7	
42 and 43	Easter Vigil	Easter Vigil	Easter Vigil [7] June 19-25
43	[26] Oct. 30-Nov. 5		
45	Annunciation	Annunciation	Annunciation
45:1-2, 6-9		[17] Aug. 28-Sept. 3	
45:10-17	[9] July 3-9		
46	Easter Vigil [4] May 29-June 4	Easter Vigil	Easter Vigil Christ the King
47	Ascension	Ascension	Ascension
48		[9] July 3-9	
49:1-12			[13] July 31-Aug. 6
50:1-6		Transfiguration	

PSALMS FOR PRAISE AND WORSHIP

PSALM	A	B	C
50:1-8, 22-23	[14] Aug. 7-13		
50:7-15	[5] June 5-11		
51:1-10			[19] Sept. 11-17
51:1-12		[13] July 31-Aug. 6 Lent 5	
51:1-17	Ash Wednesday	Ash Wednesday	Ash Wednesday
52			[11] July 17-23
54		[20] Sept. 18-24	
62:5-12		Epiphany 3	
63:1-8			Lent 3
65:(1-8),9-13	[10] July 10-16		
65	Thanksgiving		[25] Oct. 23-29
66:1-9			[9] July 3-9
66:1-12			[23] Oct. 9-15
66:8-20	Easter 6		
67	[15] Aug. 14-20		Easter 6
68:1-10, 32-35	Easter 7		
69:7-10, (11-15),16-18	[7] June 19-25		
70	[27] Nov. 6-12		
71:1-6			Epiphany 4 [16] Aug. 21-27
71:1-14	Tuesday in Holy Week	Tuesday in Holy Week	Tuesday in Holy Week
72:1-7, 10-14	Epiphany	Epiphany	Epiphany
72:1-7, 18-19	Advent 2		

PSALMS FOR PRAISE AND WORSHIP

PSALM	A	B	C
90:1-8, (9-11), 12	[28] Nov. 13-19		
90:1-6, 13-17	[25] Oct. 23-29		
90:12-17		[23] Oct. 9-15	
91:1-2, 9-16			Lent 1
91:1-6, 14-16		[21] Sept. 25-Oct. 1	
91:9-16		[24] Oct. 16-22	
92:1-4, 12-15		Epiphany 8 [6] June 12-18	
93		Ascension Christ the King	
95:1-7a	Christ the King		
95	Lent 3		
96:1-9, (10-13)	[24] Oct. 16-22		
96	Christmas Eve	Christmas Eve	Christmas Eve [4] May 29-June 4
97	Christmas Day	Christmas Day	Christmas Day Easter 7
98:1-5	Holy Cross	Holy Cross	Holy Cross
98	Christmas Day Easter Vigil	Christmas Day Easter Vigil Easter 6	Christmas Day Easter Vigil [27] Nov. 6-12 [28] Nov. 13-19
99	Transfiguration [24] Oct. 16-22		Transfiguration
100	[6] June 12-18 Christ the King		Thanksgiving
103:1-8			
103: (1-7), 8-13	[19] Sept. 11-17		[16] Aug. 21-27

PSALM	A	B	C
103:1-13, 22		Epiphany 8	
104:1-9,24, 35c	[24] Oct. 16-22		
104:24-34, 35b	Pentecost	Pentecost	Pentecost
105:1-6, 16-22, 45b	[14] Aug. 7-13		
105:1-11, 45b	[12] July 24-30		
105:1-6, 23-26, 45c	[17] Aug. 28-Sept. 3		
105:1-6, 37-45	[20] Sept. 18-24		
106:1-6, 19-23	[21] Oct. 9-15		
107:1-3,17-22	Lent 4		
107:1-3,23-32	[7] June 19-25		
107:1-7, 33-37	[26] Oct. 30-Nov. 5		
107:1-9, 43			[13] July 31-Aug. 6
110			Ascension
111		Epiphany 4 [15] Aug. 14-20	[23] Oct. 9-15
112:1-9, (10)	Epiphany 5		
112			[17] Aug. 28-Sept. 3
113	Visitation	Visitation	Visitation [20] Sept. 18-24
114	Easter Vigil Easter Evening [14] Sept. 11-17	Easter Vigil Easter Evening	Easter Vigil Easter Evening
116:1-9		[19] Sept. 11-17	
116:1-2, 12-19	Holy Thursday [6] June 12-18	Holy Thursday	Holy Thursday
116:1-4, 12-19	Easter 3		

PSALMS FOR PRAISE AND WORSHIP

PSALM	A	B	C
118:1-2, 14-24	Easter	Easter	Easter
118:1-2, 19-29	Passion/Palm Sunday	Passion/Palm Sunday	Passion/Palm Sunday
118:14-29			Easter 2
119:1-8	Epiphany 6	[26] Oct. 30-Nov. 5	
119:9-16		Lent 5	
119:33-40	Epiphany 7 [18] Sept. 4-10		
119:97-104			[24] Oct. 16-22
119:105-112	[10] July 10-16		
119:129-136	[12] July 24-30		
119:137-144			[26] Oct. 30-Nov. 5
121	Lent 2		[24] Oct. 16-22
122	Advent 1		
123	[28] Nov. 13-19	[9] July 3-9	
124	[16] Aug. 21-17	[21] Sept. 25-Oct. 1	
125		[18] Sept. 4-10	
126		Advent 3 [25] Oct. 23-29 Thanksgiving	Lent 5
127		[27] Nov. 6-12	
128	[12] July 24-30		
130	Lent 5	[5] June 5-11 [8] June 26-July 2 [14] Aug. 7-13	
131	Epiphany 8		
132:1-12, (13-18)		Christ the King	

PSALM	A	B	C
133	[15] Aug. 14-20	Easter 2 [7] June 19-25	
136:1-9, 23-26	Easter Vigil	Easter Vigil	Easter Vigil
137			[22] Oct. 2-8
138	[16] Aug. 21-27	[8] June 5-11	Epiphany 5 [12] July 24-30
139:1-6, 13-18	Epiphany 2	[4] May 29-June 4	[18] Sept. 4-10
139:1-12, 23-24	[11] July 17-23		
143	Easter Vigil	Easter Vigil	Easter Vigil
145:1-8	[20] Sept. 18-24		
145:1-5, 17-21		[27] Nov. 6-12	
145:8-14	[9] July 3-9		
145:8-9, 14-21	[13] July 31-Aug. 6		
145:10-18		[12] July 24-30	
146		[18] Sept. 4-10 [26] Oct. 30-Nov. 5 [27] Nov. 6-12	[5] June 5-11 [21] Sept. 25-Oct. 1
146:5-10	Advent 3		
147:1-11, 20c		Epiphany 5	
147:12-20	2 after Christmas	2 after Christmas	2 after Christmas
148	1 after Christmas	1 after Christmas	1 after Christmas Easter 5
149	[18] Sept. 4-10		All Saints
150			Easter 2

Index of Psalms
for Sundays and Special Days

DAY	A	B	C
Advent 1	122	80:1-7, 17-19	25:1-10
Advent 2	72:1-7, 18-19	85:1-2, 8-13	
Advent 3	146:5-10	126	
Advent 4	80:1-7, 17-19	89:1-4, 19-26	80:1-7
Christmas Eve	96	96	96
Nativity of the Lord			
(Christmas Day)	97, 98	97, 98	97, 98
Christmas 1 (or Epiphany)	148	148	148
January 1 (New Year)	8, 117	8	8, 90:1-2
January 1 Holy Name	8, 67	8, 67	8,67
Christmas 2	147:12-20	147:12-20	147:12-20
Epiphany 1	72:1-7, 10-14	72:1-7, 10-14	72:1-7, 10-14
Baptism of the Lord	29	29	29
Epiphany 2	40:1-11	139:1-6, 13-18	36:5-10
Epiphany 3	27:1, 4-9	62:5-12	19
Epiphany 4	15	111	71:1-6
Epiphany 5	112:1-9 (10)	147:1-11, 20c	138
Epiphany 6	119:1-8	30	1
Epiphany 7	119:33-40	41	37:1-11
Epiphany 8	131	103:1-13, 22	92:1-4, 12-15
Last Sunday after Epiphany	2, 99	50:1-6	99
(Transfiguration)			
Ash Wednesday	51:1-17	51:1-17	51:1-17
Lent 1	32	25:1-10	91:1-2, 9-16
Lent 2	121	22:23-31	27
Lent 3	95	19	63:1-8
Lent 4	23	107:1-3, 17-22	32
Lent 5	130	51:1-12; 126	119:9-16
Lent 6, Passion/	31:9-16;	31:9-16	31:9-16
Palm Sunday	118:1-2, 19-29	118:1-2, 19-29	118:1-2, 19-29
Monday of Holy Week	36:5-10	36:5-10	36:5-10
Tuesday of Holy Week	71:1-14	71:1-14	71:1-14
Wednesday of Holy Week	70	70	70
Holy Thursday	116:1-2, 12-19	116:1-2, 12-19	116:1-2, 12-19
Good Friday	22	22	22
Holy Saturday	31:1-4, 15-16	31:1-4, 15-16	31:1-4, 15-16
Easter Vigil	16; 19; 42; 43;	16; 19; 42; 43;	16; 19; 42; 43;
	46; 98; 114;	46; 98; 114;	46; 98; 114;
	136:1-9,23-26;	136:1-9,23-26;	136:1-9,23-26;
	143	143	143
Easter	118:14-24	118:14-24	118:14-24

PSALMS FOR PRAISE AND WORSHIP

DAY	A	B	C
Easter Evening	114, 150	114, 150	114, 118:14-24,
Easter 2	16	118:14-29; 133	150
Easter 3	116:1-4, 12-19	4	30
Easter 4	23	23	23
Easter 5	31:1-5, 15-16	22:25-31	148
Easter 6	66:8-20	98	67
Ascension	47	47, 93	47, 110
Easter 7	68:1-10, 32-35	1	97
Pentecost	104:24-34, 35b	104:24-34, 35b	104:24-34,35b
Trinity	8	29	8
Sunday between May 29 and June 4 inclusive (if after Trinity Sunday)	31:1-5, 19-24; 46	81:1-10; 139:1-6, 13-18	96; 96:1-9
Sunday between June 5 and June 11 inclusive (if after Trinity Sunday)	33:1-12; 50:7-15	130; 138	30; 146
Sunday between June 12 and June 18 inclusive (if after Trinity Sunday)	100; 116:1-2, 12-19	20; 92:1-4, 12-15	5:1-8; 32
Sunday between June 19 and June 25 inclusive (if after Trinity Sunday)	69:7-10, (11-15), 16-18; 86:1-10, 16-17	9:9-20; 107:1-3, 23-32	22:19-28; 42 and 43
Sunday between June 26 and July 2 inclusive	13; 89:1-4, 15-18	30; 130	16; 77:1-2, 11-20
Sunday between July 3 and July 9 inclusive	45:10-17; 145:8-14	48; 143	30; 66:1-9
Sunday between July 10 and July 16 inclusive	65:(1-8), 9-13; 119:105-112	24; 85:8-13	25:1-10; 82
Sunday between July 17 and July 23 inclusive	86:11-17; 139:1-12; 23-24	23; 89:20-37	15; 52
Sunday between July 24 and July 30 inclusive	105:1-11, 45b; 119:129-136; 128	14; 145:10-18	85:138
Sunday between July 31 and August 6 inclusive	17:1-7, 15; 145:8-9, 14-21	51:1-12; 78:23-29	49:1-12; 107:1-9, 43
Sunday between August 7 and August 13 inclusive	85:8-13; 105:1-6, 16-22, 45b	34:1-8; 130	33:12-22; 50:1-8, 22-23
Sunday between August 14 and August 20 inclusive	67; 133	34:9-14; 111	80:1-2, 8-19 82

INDEX OF PSALMS FOR SUNDAYS AND SPECIAL DAYS

DAY	A	B	C
Sunday between August 21 and August 27 inclusive	124; 138	34:15-22; 84	71:1-6; 103:1-8
Sunday between August 28 and September 3 inclusive	26:1-8; 105:1-6, 23-26, 45c	15; 45:1-2, 6-9	81:1, 10-16; 112
Sunday between September 4 and September 10 inclusive	119:33-40; 149	125; 146	1; 139:1-6, 13-18
Sunday between September 11 and September 17 inclusive	103:(1-7), 8-13; 114	19; 116:1-9	14; 51:1-10
Sunday between September 18 and September 24 inclusive	105:1-6, 37-45; 145:1-8	1; 54	79:1-9; 113
Sunday between September 25 and October 1 inclusive	25:1-9; 78:1-4, 12-16	19:7-14; 124	91:1-6, 14-16; 146
Sunday between October 2 and October 8 inclusive	19; 80:7-15	8; 26	37:1-9; 137
Sunday between October 9 and October 15 inclusive	23; 106:1-6, 19-23	22:1-15; 90:12-17	66:1-12; 111
Sunday between October 16 and October 22 inclusive	96:1-9, (10-13); 99	91:9-16; 104:1-9, 24, 35c	119:97-104; 121
Sunday between October 23 and October 29 inclusive	1; 90:1-6, 13-17	34:1-8, (19-22); 126	65; 84:1-7
Sunday between October 30 and November 5 inclusive	43; 107:1-7, 33-37	119:1-8; 146	32:1-7; 119:137-144
Sunday between November 6 and November 12 inclusive	70; 78:1-7	127; 146	17:1-9; 98; 145:1-5, 17-21
Sunday between November 13 and November 19 inclusive	90:1-8, (9-11), 12; 123	16	98
Presentation	24:7-10; 84	24:7-10; 84	24:7-10; 84
Annunciation	40:5-10; 45	40:5-10; 45	40:5-10; 45
Visitation	113	113	113
Holy Cross	78:1-2, 34-38; 98:1-5	78:1-2, 34-38; 98:1-5	78:1-2, 34-38; 98:1-5
All Saints	34:1-10, 22	24	149
Thanksgiving Day	65	126	100
Christ the King (Sunday occurring Nov. 20 to 26)	95:1-7a; 100	93; 132:1-12, (13-18)	46

Index of Responses
by First Line

(The number at the end of each Response text is the number of the Response found on pages 179-234.)

I shall walk at liberty,
  for I have sought your precepts. (92)
I sing of your promise, O Lord, your
  faithfulness to all generations. (100)
I sing your praise for steadfast love;
  fulfill your purpose for me. (47)
I will give you as a light to the nations,
  my salvation to the ends of the
    earth. (53)
In despair I cry to the Lord;
  O Lord, come to my aid. (124)
In my distress I cry to the Lord:
  "Deliver me, O Lord." (99)
In our distress we cry to you;
  come, Lord, and set us free! (76)
Joy to the world! the Lord is come. (73)
Justice alone is the way of the Lord;
  be just and worship God. (13)
Lead me, Lord, lead me in thy
  righteousness; make thy way plain
    before my face. (24)
Let all things their creator bless:
  Alleluia! Alleluia! Alleluia! (30)
Let all who take refuge in you rejoice,
  let them ever sing for joy. (7)
Let justice roll down like waters, and
  righteousness like flowing streams.
    (55)
Let us see your kindness, Lord;
  grant us your salvation. (101)
Light rises in darkness when justice
  rules our lives. (84)
Like a tree that's planted by the water,
  we shall not be moved. (2)
Lord, make me to know your ways.
  Lead me in your truth, and teach
    me. (23)
Lord of all, to thee we raise
  this our hymn of grateful praise. (80)
Lord, renew us in love and sacrifice;
  Alpha and Omega be. (90)
Make joyful noise, lift up your voice!
  Ye nations of the earth, rejoice! (75)
Many and great, O God, are thy things,
  Maker of earth and sky. (9)
My hope is lost; breathe life upon me.
    (12)
My soul longs for your courts, O Lord;
  in your presence is fullness of joy. (61)
Now, O Lord, for what do I wait?

For my hope is in you alone. (36)
Now thank we all our God
  with heart and hands and voices.(48)
O come, thou Wisdom from on high,
  and order all things far and nigh.
    (110)
O God, arise and judge the earth,
  for to you belong all nations. (119)
O Lord, do not withhold your mercy;
  let your steadfast love preserve me.
    (37)
O Lord, you are my hope,
  my trust, Lord, from my youth. (52)
O Lord, your love is constant;
  you are faithful to all generations.(64)
O magnify the Lord with me;
  with me exalt God's name! (34)
O people, be glad and sing for joy!
  Declare God's glory in every land!
    (49)
O praise the Lord, who delivers your
  soul from death. (88)
O sacred Head, now wounded, with
  grief and shame weighed down. (18)
O taste and see that the Lord is good!
  Happy are those who take refuge in
    God! (33)
Our soul waits for the Lord,
  who is our help and shield. (32)
Out of the depths I cry to thee;
  Lord, hear me, I implore thee! (51)
Praise the Lord, praise the Lord,
  for God has visited and redeemed us.
    (85)
Praise to the Lord, the Almighty,
  who rules all creation. (78)
Praise the Lord who reigns above:
  Alleluia! (114)
Praise the Lord, ye saints, and sing;
  all the powers of music bring. (112)
Pray for the peace of Jerusalem;
  within your walls be peace. (96)
Preserve me, O God, for in you I take
  refuge. (14)
Rejoice, rejoice, rejoice, give thanks, and
  sing. (74)
Remember the wonderful works of the
  Lord! Praise God, give thanks, and
    sing! (56)

Index of Composers and Authors

Numbers refer to response numbers; see pages 179-234.

Selected Bibliography

I. CRITICAL STUDY OF THE PSALMS

Brueggemann, Walter, *The Message of the Psalms*, Minneapolis: Augsburg, 1984.

Dahood, Mitchell, *Psalms I, II, III*, New York: Doubleday, 1965-70.

Miller, Patrick D., *Interpreting the Psalms*, Philadelphia: Fortress, 1986.

Mowinckel, Sigmund, *The Psalms in Israel's Worship*, 2 vols., Nashville: Abingdon, 1967.

Shepherd, Massey H., *Psalms in Christian Worship*, Minneapolis: Augsburg, 1976.

Weiser, Artur, *The Psalms*, Philadelphia: Westminster, 1962.

Westermann, Claus, *The Praise of God in the Psalms*, Richmond: John Knox, 1965.

II. PSALM COLLECTIONS

Barrett, James C., *The Psalmnary: Gradual Psalms for Cantor and Congregation*, Missoula, Mont: Hymnary Press, 1982.

Gelineau, Joseph, *The Psalms: A New Translation from the Hebrew Arranged for Singing*, Glasgow: Collins, 1980.

Gradual Psalms I, II, III, New York: Church Hymnal Corporation, 1980-1989.

Haas, David, *Psalms for the Church Year*, Chicago: G.I.A., 1983.

Isele, David Clark, *Psalms for the Church Year*, Chicago: G.I.A., 1979.

Litton, James, ed., *Plainsong Psalter*, Episcopal Church, Standing Commission on Church Music, New York: Church Hymnal Corporation, 1988.

Melloh, S.A. and Joncas, Michael, eds., *Praise God in Song*, Chicago: G.I.A., 1979.

Peloquin, A., *Songs of Israel*, Chicago: G.I.A., 1971.

A Responsorial Psalm Book: The responsorial psalms from the 3-year lectionary cycle for Sundays and feastdays, London: Collins, 1980.

Shepherd, Massey H., *A Liturgical Psalter for the Christian Year*, Collegeville, Minn.: Augsburg, 1976.

Webber, Christopher L., *A New Metrical Psalter*, New York: Church Hymnal Corporation, 1986.

III. SINGING THE PSALMS

Anderson, Fred R., *Singing Psalms of Joy and Praise*, Philadelphia: Westminster, 1986.

Hopson, Hal, *Psalm Refrains and Tones*, Carol Stream, Ill.: Hope, 1957.

Pierik, Marie, *The Psalter in the Temple and the Church*, Washington: Catholic University Press, 1957.

Vogel, Dwight W., *Singing the Psalms*, Nashville: Discipleship Resources, 1991.

Willan, Healy, ed., *The Canadian Psalter, Plainsong Edition*, Toronto: John Deyell Co., 1963, 1973, 1984.

Wyton, Alec, ed., *The Anglican Chant Psalter*, New York: Church Hymnal Corporation, 1987.